THE BASICS BOOK

of Information Networking

Motorola Codex

**MOTOROLA
UNIVERSITY
PRESS**

ADDISON-WESLEY PUBLISHING COMPANY, INC.
Reading, Massachusetts · Menlo Park, California · New York
Don Mills, Ontario · Wokingham, England · Amsterdam
Bonn · Paris · Milan · Madrid · Sydney
Singapore · Tokyo · Seoul · Taipei
Mexico City · San Juan

The publisher offers discounts on this book when ordered
in quantity for special sales. For more information please
contact:

Corporate & Professional Publishing Group
Addison-Wesley Publishing Company
Route 128
Reading, Massachusetts 01867

ISBN: 0-201-56370-3

1 2 3 4 5 6 7 8 9 10   MW   9594939291

First printing, November, 1991

MOTOROLA UNIVERSITY PRESS

The Motorola Codex Basics Book Series
The Basics Book of Information Networking
The Basics Book of X.25 Packet Switching
The Basics Book of ISDN
The Basics Book of OSI and Network Management
The Basics Book of Frame Relaying

WORLD HEADQUARTERS
20 Cabot Boulevard
Mansfield, Massachusetts USA 02048-1193
Tel: (508) 261-4000, Fax: (508) 337-8004

SELECTED WORLDWIDE LOCATIONS
Belgium:
SA Motorola NV, Brussels
    Tel: 32 (2) 718-5411
Canada:
Motorola Information Systems, Brampton, Ontario
    Tel: (416) 507-7200
France:
Motorola Codex Systemes D'Information, Paris
    Tel: 33(1) 4664-1680
Germany:
Motorola GMBH, Darmstadt
    Tel: 49 (6151) 8807-0
Hong Kong:
Motorola Asia Ltd., Causeway Bay
    Tel: 852 887-8335
Ireland:
Motorola Codex, Dublin
    Tel: 353 (1) 426-711
Israel:
Motorola Israel Information Systems Ltd., Tel-Aviv
    Tel: 972 (3) 751-8333
Japan:
Nippon Motorola Ltd., Tokyo
    Tel: 81 (3) 3440-3311
Spain:
Motorola Codex Spain, Madrid
    Tel: 34 (1) 634-0384
Sweden:
Motorola AB Codex Datacommunications Sector, Stockholm
    Tel: 46 (8) 795-9980
United Kingdom:
Motorola Codex, Wallington
    Tel: 44 (81) 669-4343
United States:
        Eastern Area, Clifton, NJ Tel: (201) 470-9001
        Southern Area, Dallas, TX Tel: (214) 690-5221
        Central Area, Schaumburg, IL Tel: (708) 576-2036
        Western Area, Long Beach, CA Tel: (310) 421-0086

PREFACE

In 1983, we published *The Basics Book of Data Communications*. Since then, the book has developed quite a following. What began as an attempt to make the subject of data communications both accessible and enjoyable has become something of an industry primer. That book, in turn, gave birth to a family of more specialized basics books on topics ranging from V.32 to ISDN.

Now, for the first time, we've substantially updated and revised the original *Basics Book*. Much that is here will be familiar. The first seven chapters of the book cover pretty much the same ground as its predecessor, but with some modification and shifts in emphasis to reflect recent trends and industry changes. The last five chapters comprise mostly new material. Here you will find discussions of digital services, X.25 networking, network topologies (including LAN and MAN), and network management, as well as some new applications.

To reflect all these changes, we've given the book a new name—*The Basics Book of Information Networking*. As before, we've kept the tone light and the information, well, basic. That's how you've liked it over the years, and we send it on its current journey in the hope that it will continue to please the readers it is designed to serve.

TABLE OF CONTENTS

INTRODUCTION

If you're one of those people who break out in a cold sweat trying to figure out the difference between a switched and dial line (they're actually the same thing), this book is for you. It might not be your job to understand how to configure a network, but knowing how to speak data communications (not exactly a romance language) is essential in your business today. As your company expands, your communications needs expand with it. And how you meet those needs in turn has an impact on future growth and profit. Speaking the "language" will help you to understand the price/performance/application relationship of information networking equipment so crucial to your organization's success.

For lack of a good understanding, companies may buy the best equipment, not anticipating incompatibility between certain products—the ensuing nightmare can be a high-tech version of the Tower of Babel. Then there are the inevitable network problems that seem to come from nowhere. When your network isn't up and running (even the best systems go down), it's everybody's concern. A little basic knowledge can save time and frustration when a network failure threatens to bring your business to a halt.

The Basics Book of Information Networking is a practical overview of communications for the "less experienced." Our intention is to make what can be a dry and difficult subject as enjoyable as words and illustrations can make it. We feel that we're in the most exciting, fast-moving industry on earth and we'd like to share our understanding and enthusiasm for its achievements with you.

Motorola Codex has been a leader in data communications and information networking for nearly 30 years. As a company providing complete networking solutions, we're in a good position to explain how the technological advancements fit into the total picture. You may not be able to configure a complex network after reading this book, but you'll be able to ask the questions necessary for properly evaluating and selecting information networking equipment.

You'll gain high-tech knowledge applicable to day-to-day business situations. And you'll be able to hold your own at any cocktail party when the subject of baud rate comes up (you might even bring it up yourself). You'll understand the concepts behind "networking"—the way in which data gets from one point to another. And you'll become familiar with the tools needed to play this somewhat advanced version of "connect the dots."

So start saving money and take a look at the next page. It won't hurt a bit (a bit has a whole different meaning in data communications, but don't panic).

BASIC
BASICS
OR

the road map

Most basic data communications books begin with a brief rundown of civilization since the abacus, as seen through the eyes of someone with three degrees in computer science. However, we're betting that you're not as interested in the past as the present. Besides, the entire history of data communications since the abacus comes down to this—to have data communications requires three important components. First, a **transmitter.** Second, a **medium** over which the data travels. And third, a **receiver.**

But what is data communications and why do we need it? The following brief explanation should leave you with questions, but don't be concerned. The rest of this book is designed to answer those questions and more.

"What" data communications is, is the movement of computer-encoded information from one point to another, by means of an electrical transmission system. The "why" is for the all important benefit of near instantaneous information exchange over long distances. The applications you see every day range from money-making to life-saving.

This communication between machines uses established codes based on the binary number system. Binary uses "zero" and "one" to represent the absence or presence of an electrical charge. To the machines, these zeros and ones represent "off/on" conditions. In various combinations, they can be used to represent anything you would ever want to transmit.

Now, a data communications network can be divided into three distinct parts. The **Data Terminal Equipment** (DTE) is any digital device such as a terminal, printer or computer that transmits and/or receives data. We call them "digital" because they operate in binary. The **Data Communications Equipment** (DCE) is any other device attached to the communications line that manipulates the transmitted signal or

Data leaves your DTE device as a digital signal and travels the phone line as an analog signal.

data (you'll see why it needs to be manipulated in a second). The third part is the medium over which the signal is sent. Often, the medium used is a telephone line.

figure 1-1

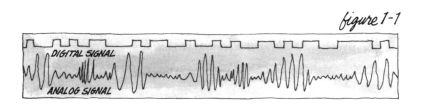

The point at which these devices connect with one another is called the **interface**. You can think of an interface as a way of translating the characteristics of one piece of equipment into the next—a shared boundary. EIA 232-D is an example of a common physical interface used to join equipment, but more on this later.

As long as we're throwing curve balls, we said DTEs work in digital. You may already know phone lines often operate in what's called **analog**. The way these two transmission signals represent the exact same data is quite different as you can see in figure 1-1.

If two digital devices want to communicate over an analog telephone line, then equipment must be added at either end to convert the digital signal to analog so it can travel the phone line, and then convert it back to digital so it can feed directly into a DTE at the receiving end. These devices that *mo*dulate and *demod*ulate or manipulate the signal are called **modems** and belong to the DCE category (figure 1-2).

So why use phone lines at all if they don't even operate in the same language as the data terminal equipment? As the first network designer once said, "Because they're there." In fact, they're everywhere. What better way to communicate with a distant

Modems convert the digital signal to analog so it can travel the phone line and then back to digital again for processing.

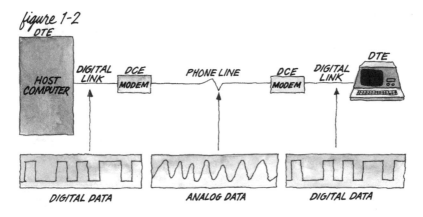

figure 1-2

DTE

HOST COMPUTER | DIGITAL LINK | DCE MODEM | PHONE LINE | DCE MODEM | DIGITAL LINK | DTE

DIGITAL DATA   ANALOG DATA   DIGITAL DATA

computer or terminal than through this incredibly vast network? Try to think of someone you'd want to transmit data to who doesn't at least have a telephone.

Previously, we said the phone lines often operate in analog. Actually, until the last twenty years, they only operated in analog. Today, high-speed **digital** circuits and services for transmitting digitally over long distances are becoming increasingly available. However, for your "road map," we'll start with the basics of analog communications where it all began and cover the newer digital services in Chapter 8.

One more digression. **Local Area Networking** provides a cost-effective alternative to phone line transmission for short-range communications. Today's LANs use their own set of twisted pair, coaxial cables or fiber optic threads to transmit data at high speeds typically over distances of one to two miles. But more on this in

A series of point-to-point networks where each DTE is linked to the host computer by its own phone line can be very expensive.

Chapter 10 when we talk about network topology.

Whether analog or digital, phone lines can be very expensive. In fact, the cost of the transmission medium could easily represent the largest part of your data communi-

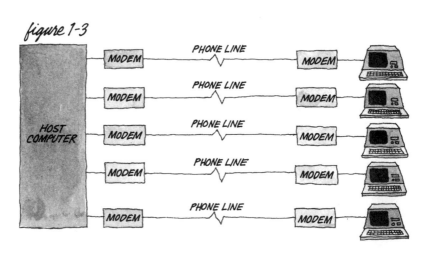

figure 1-3

HOST COMPUTER

MODEM — PHONE LINE — MODEM

MODEM — PHONE LINE — MODEM

MODEM — PHONE LINE — MODEM

MODEM — PHONE LINE — MODEM

MODEM — PHONE LINE — MODEM

cations budget. You essentially have two choices: to **lease** specific phone lines for your exclusive use at a flat monthly rate, or to use the regular telephone or **dial** network and make individual phone calls to the receiving DTE each time you want to transmit data.

Which alternative you choose will depend on how often, how far, and how fast you want to transmit your data. Another factor in your decision is whether your terminals are geographically dispersed or co-located near the computer facility.

Although we'll discuss selecting transmission lines in more detail, you can already see that as you add more DTEs to your network, the cost of repeating a series of **point-to-point** networks, where each DTE is linked to the computer by its own phone line, can be astronomical (figure 1-3).

The solution in some instances is to redesign or reconfigure the network into a **multipoint** network, where several DTEs share

One solution for reducing line and modem costs is a multipoint network where several DTEs share the same phone line. In this case, we've been able to eliminate four phone lines and four modems.

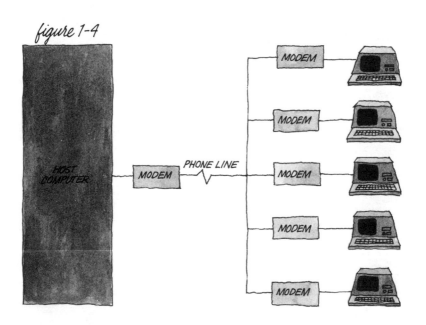

figure 1-4

5

the same line as illustrated in figure 1-4. This saves you the expense of separate phone lines between each DTE and the computer. In other network environments, **multiplexers** can eliminate the need for a number of parallel phone lines. Rather than five separate phone lines for your five terminals, you use only one line by putting a multiplexer at each end. These devices merge all five digital links at one end and then sort them out again at their destination. This way, one phone line serves many terminals (figure 1-5).

Multiplexers can also eliminate a number of parallel phone lines by merging the digital links at one end and sorting them out at their destination. In this case, we've reduced the network shown in figure 1-3 by four phone lines and eight modems.

Another word to remember is **protocol**. It's just what it sounds like—the ground rules. Protocols in data communications are the procedures required to initiate and maintain communication. For your data, protocols can be thought of as the rules of the road—not the content of the data but rather how it's "packaged" for travel.

One aspect of protocols describes how data moves directionally over the telephone lines. There are three methods—simplex, half-duplex and full-duplex (figure 1-6).

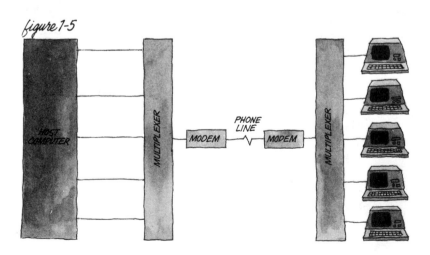

figure 1-5

HOST COMPUTER — MULTIPLEXER — MODEM — PHONE LINE — MODEM — MULTIPLEXER

Your choice depends on what application you're fulfilling, what lines are available and the costs involved.

Briefly, phone lines come in two varieties, **two-wire** and **four-wire**. Dial lines are two-wire; one to carry the signal, while the other acts as a "return" to complete the circuit. Leased lines are generally four-wire, offering two independent communication paths.

In **simplex** transmission, data flows in only one direction. This mode is hardly ever used because most data communications applications require some kind of response from the receiving end to indicate that the data arrived intact. An example of simplex is listening to your radio—unless you're having a bad day, you're not responding.

In **half-duplex** transmission, data flows in both directions but, the catch is, in only one direction at a time. A factor in half-duplex transmissions is **line turnaround**—the time required for the line to "clear" before transmitting in the other direction. This of course wastes some time. Half-duplex operates over either two- or four-wire lines. One advantage of using four-wire is decreased turnaround time.

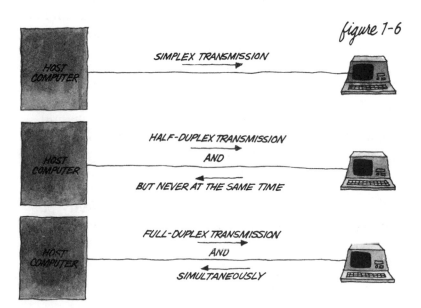

figure 1-6

SIMPLEX TRANSMISSION

HALF-DUPLEX TRANSMISSION
AND
BUT NEVER AT THE SAME TIME

FULL-DUPLEX TRANSMISSION
AND
SIMULTANEOUSLY

Imagine a railroad that uses a single track. A train would have to be removed from the track at its destination before another train could be sent in the opposite direction. This illustrates half-duplex transmission over two-wires (remember only one wire actually carries the signal).

For a four-wire, half-duplex line, we expand the analogy to two tracks, one for each direction. One train still can't leave until the other has arrived but this procedure wastes less time compared to trying to clear a single track for two-way travel.

Full-duplex permits simultaneous transmission in both directions. Full-duplex, however, requires two separate transmission paths, one for each direction. This is accomplished by operating over four-wire lines or using special modems to split the transmission channel of a dial, two-wire line to create two independent communication paths. Pursuing the train analogy, we now have two parallel tracks, one for each direction, and trains on one track run without regard to trains on the other track. This represents a somewhat faster, more efficient method of transmitting data.

Finally, ever try plugging a three-prong electrical plug into a two-prong outlet? This is a good illustration of mixing **standards** and the desired convenience of having one standard. Now multiply that little inconvenience by about a million and you'll understand what it could be like dealing with different data communications vendors if they don't design compatible products according to accepted guidelines.

Whether sending data across a city or around the world, the goal is for different products to work together **transparently** so you feel like you're dealing directly with the DTE at the other end, not the data-comm products in between. And it is only the existence of standards that makes this kind of **connectivity** possible—from communication between two points to the ability to expand your network worldwide as your business demands.

Right now in the industry, standards aren't very standard. Rather than one universal communications standard, there are competing models. To complicate the standards process further, U.S. standards are frequently incompatible with foreign standards. Today, it rests upon the data communications vendors to select the standard they believe will eventually gain acceptance, and design their product line around those specifications.

Standards develop in a couple of ways. "De facto" standards, like IBM's Systems Network Architecture (SNA) and all of AT&T's standards, are the result of large organizations developing preferred solutions through their resources and influence (in other words, you want to play on their team, you play by their rules). In other cases, standards are formed by committees established to evaluate recommendations from private industry and public organizations such as European telephone companies.

For example, the **OSI** (Open Systems Interconnection) **Basic Reference Model** developed by the **International Organization for Standardization** (ISO) is gaining acceptance throughout the world today for its flexibility. We'll have a lot more to say about OSI in Chapter 9.

What's important to remember about open standards is that they facilitate integration, choice, and flexibility by allowing you to design your network and easily add products from different vendors to meet your business requirements. They're good for you and good for the vendors.

Congratulations. You've just successfully passed the fastest basic data communications course in the high tech world. We apologize for going so quickly but we needed to create a total framework that the following chapters will elaborate on. Using Chapter 1 as your road map, we'll start back at square one. There's a computer out there somewhere and you want to communicate with it.

2

A FEW WORDS ABOUT TERMINALS

OR

one size does not fit all

To communicate with a computer, you need an input device of some kind (like a keyboard). As we mentioned, DTEs cover a range of equipment from the host computer itself, which is also known as the mainframe or central processing unit (CPU), to input/output devices like terminals, printers, and now even fax machines. For the purposes of this chapter we're limiting our discussion of terminals to interactive or conversational devices with either soft-copy output via a display screen, hard-copy output via a printer, or both. You can think of them simply as the remote equivalent of computer room input/output devices attached to a communications line (figure 2-1).

In a broad sense, the terminal is the interface between your business and the data communications network. And in some cases, it may be the only visible evidence that you are indeed linked to such a network.

So how fast, reliable, and "friendly" you find data communications to be, will be deeply colored by your experience with the terminal.

A bad "terminal" experience caused by choosing the wrong device for your application could lead to hair pulling, name calling, tense relationships and the feeling that the entire data communications industry is for the birds (as evidenced by the strong attraction birds have for phone lines). Not only that, but a poor choice could reduce the overall efficiency of your network by slowing the system down and increasing overall costs.

Correctly matching the terminal to the task and the characteristics of an existing network requires careful investigation. This is why we say "one size does not fit all."

There is such a variety of terminals today that at first glance, the range of products seems only second to that of snowflakes. This range is extended even further by the modular design of many terminals, allowing you to add peripherals.

A few of the many DTE devices available today.

figure 2-1

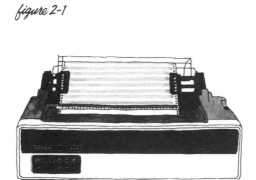

12

erals like extra memory and other devices to modify them for new applications. In addition, vendors define categories of terminals differently so even if classification names are similar, the range of features may vary.

A consideration in choosing a terminal for communications is the amount of built-in intelligence the device has. The cost of the device can be proportional to the intelligence. So "the smarter, the better" is not necessarily true, especially if you're paying for intelligence you don't need. The application should determine the amount of terminal intelligence required.

DUMB TERMINALS

On the low end of the price/performance scale are dumb terminals. Generally, these low speed devices transmit in an **asynchronous** mode where characters travel individually down the line as they are keyed in by the operator. Since no one types at a constant rate, these characters travel the line at irregular intervals. We'll discuss asynchronous and synchronous transmissions more thoroughly in Chapter 3 but you can see that wasted time between characters means fewer characters will be transmitted within a given time (figure 2-2).

Dumb terminals transmit asynchronously, which means characters travel the communications line at irregular intervals as they are keyed in.

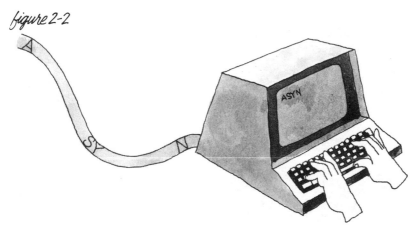

figure 2-2

13

A dumb terminal usually doesn't have the capability to be "addressable." Without an address, it can't tell when the computer is selecting it from among other terminals to either transmit or receive data—a procedure called **polling**. This precludes it from being connected with other dumb terminals to the same line.

Dumb asynchronous terminals often lack full **error-checking** capability which is a way of making sure data arrives without errors that can occur during transmission. This can be more important for certain applications, particularly when DTEs are linked by phone lines. An error in straight text transmission isn't as critical where the meaning is still obvious, but in a printout of your bank statement, a misplaced zero could have serious consequences.

So who uses dumb terminals and why? Dumb asynchronous terminals are generally associated with minicomputer environments which also operate asynchronously. In minicomputer networks, the terminals

Dumb terminals are by definition "interactive direct-connect"—one terminal per communications line.

are often located near the processor so phone line links are less commonly used. Avoiding phone line transmission also avoids transmission errors associated with phone

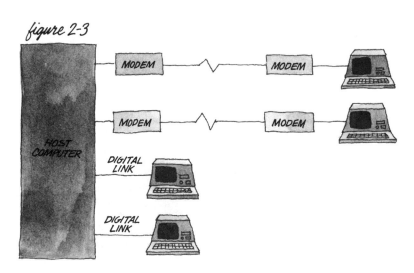

figure 2-3

MODEM — MODEM

MODEM — MODEM

HOST COMPUTER

DIGITAL LINK

DIGITAL LINK

line disturbances, making error protection less of a factor. And if dumb terminals use individual, hardwired direct digital links, they don't need the extra intelligence required for line sharing capabilities or polling.

In fact, dumb terminals by definition are "interactive direct connect"—one terminal per communication line (figure 2-3). We'll discuss this again in Chapters 6 and 7 but there's one exception to this rule. Certain kinds of multiplexers allow dumb terminals to be "clustered" together and individually addressed. Plus, they perform error-checking for terminals lacking the built-in capability.

SMART AND INTELLIGENT TERMINALS

People often confuse these two categories and use the terms "smart" and "intelligent" interchangeably. Generally, both categories are associated with high-speed, **synchronous** devices that transmit entire blocks of data rather than individual characters (figure 2-4). Briefly, the difference between these two terminal groups is that "intelligent" is smarter than "smart."

Smart terminals are not user-programmable but may have limited processing capability such as editing. This means that, in general, you cannot alter the tasks that the

Synchronous terminals generally transmit entire blocks of data rather than individual characters.

figure 2-4

SYNCHRONOUS TRANSMISSION

SYNCHRONOUS TRANSMISSIONS

terminal was designed to perform and the terminal relies on the host computer's processing power for manipulating the data.

Intelligent terminals, on the other hand, accept programs written by the user and process data with little assistance from the host. In fact, you can think of an intelligent terminal as a microcomputer that only talks to the host for greater processing power or to access a central database (a pool of stored information).

The more intelligent the terminal, the more functions it can perform without tapping the resources of the host. Rather than handling the terminals' data, the host is free to do other things that make more efficient use of its power. Also, cutting down on host computer overhead allows the computer to accommodate more terminals on a multipoint or shared line. And if your terminals are connected to the computer via point-to-point dial lines (where you pay for each call), the more processing the terminals can do without calling the host, the lower the line usage costs.

Both smart and intelligent terminals also reduce transmission errors through error-checking and the ability to automatically retransmit-on-error in case a message is not received intact on the other end.

In the past, when people talked about smart and intelligent terminals, they were describing high speed, synchronous devices. But technology is moving at such an incredible rate that there are few absolutes anymore. Though personal computers, or PCs, look like terminals, they're not. PCs are actually software driven, programmable, intelligent microcomputers that can interface with either sync or async devices. Since they're programmable, PCs can be made to emulate a terminal as required for host access.

PCs are equipped with an interface to accommodate a modem and the software necessary for data communications. **Software** is the program or set of instructions written in computer language that allows the PC to communicate with a specific host. Adding on other communications capabilities like error protection through software is relatively inexpensive to do since programs are flexible and can be easily changed.

Now that there are so many devices to choose from, it's important that you first define your application, the format of data that the host will handle (asynchronous or synchronous), and the intelligence necessary to process the information. It is on this basis that you select a terminal.

What are some of the drawbacks of putting intelligence into the "field"? First is the cost involved. The benefits of reduced host overhead, better line utilization and improved operator efficiency may not necessarily offset or justify your investment. And these devices may require more complex maintenance, diagnostic procedures, vendor support, and data processing staff.

BUFFERS

Buffers can be thought of as a type of memory. Within a terminal, a buffer can store information as small as a character and as large as an entire message, depending on its size. Though some asynchronous terminals have buffers, they're normally associated with synchronous devices.

Buffered terminals appear to be transmitting simultaneously, although the data is actually being collected in the terminals' buffers and routed to the host's buffer in an orderly fashion.

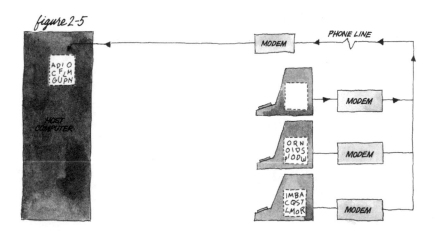

figure 2-5

The computer is capable of transmitting data at an extraordinary rate—faster than any terminal or printer can handle. It would be inefficient to slow the computer down to the speed of the DTEs. So buffers are added to both the computer and the DTEs to absorb the difference in transfer rates.

Rather than the data being transmitted character by character as it's keyed in, it collects in the terminal's buffer first. At a certain point, the buffer dumps the accumulated data onto the line where it is transmitted to the computer. The data then collects in the computer's buffer until that buffer fills to a particular level when it's worth the computer's processing time. All this may seem like a lengthy process, but to the terminal operator, it appears instantaneous.

Terminals also require buffers when more than one device is attached to the same line. All the terminals appear to be transmitting simultaneously while the data is actually being collected and routed in an orderly fashion. It is the terminal's ability to identify its own data through addressing that makes this orderly collection and distribution of data possible. Using buffers at both ends of the line keeps the computer from being tied up with any one terminal (figure 2-5).

We've just contrasted the main terminal types. Figure 2-6 is a more detailed chart, listing these groups of terminals, categorized by processing power and applications.

Since different vendors have different names for similar kinds of terminals, this chart will help you understand and be able to describe the features you require in a terminal. It's then a process of finding the vendor with the particular terminal that includes those features.

It's clear that terminals range from simple, low-cost teleprinters to expensive, sophisticated stand-alone processors. Of course, there's a lot more that can be said about terminals, but hopefully now you're somewhat less confused by the vast array.

figure 2-6

DUMB TERMINALS
☐ On the lowest end of the terminal products scale are dumb, asynchronous, interactive devices. These terminals cannot be polled, cannot acknowledge that they have received data without errors, and have no memory. This means that even though errors can be detected through parity checking (discussed in Chapter 3), these devices have no automatic retransmission-on-error.

SMART TERMINALS
☐ This second group of terminals has semiconductor-based memory, so it can be polled. These devices can also store data in blocks and send acknowledgments back as to whether the data was received and if there are errors. And because they have memory and access to processing power, if errors are found, the data can be retransmitted without having to physically key in the data a second time. Vendor supplied firmware (software on a chip) is built into these terminals for specific unalterable functions like screen formats and editing.

INTELLIGENT TERMINALS
☐ This group of terminals has all the characteristics of the last group plus vendor-supplied software that can be altered by the user for more specific applications. Terminals that are user-programmable also accept programs you write yourself. These application programs make processing possible at remote sites. Software for local storage is provided on media such as tape cassettes and floppy disks in addition to firmware that resides internally. With greater main memory plus extensive processing power, these terminals can greatly reduce host overhead. In fact, many intelligent terminals like personal computers can operate as stand-alone computers, entirely independent of a host.

You compile a list of your requirements and it turns out a leading manufacturer offers a terminal that meets all your needs. But what "language" does the terminal operate in? Is it a language the other DTEs and the computer in the network understand? And once the terminal is hooked up, is there any way of knowing your transmissions are being received? Without these answers (they're all in Chapter 3), you may find that the only one you can transmit to is yourself and you're not even sure if you're being received.

3

UNDERSTANDING LINE MANAGEMENT

OR

the rules of the road

To the newcomer, all data communications buzzwords seem to be one syllable beginning with the letter "B." Not so, but surprisingly enough, the important ones at this point are.

Bit is actually a contraction for the term "binary digit". It's the smallest unit of information used in a data communications system and is represented by either a zero or a one. Tidbit is the smallest unit of gossip used in analog phone conversations. Just kidding.

Byte is simply a grouping of bits. A byte may or may not be directly translatable into information meaningful to the user. The number of bits in a byte is determined by what the particular communication equipment is designed to handle. Eight is the most common number.

Character is not a one syllable word beginning with the letter "B". It's actually a grouping of bits similar to a byte except that it can always be translated directly into a letter, number, or punctuation mark.

Block is a set of bits and/or bytes which represent a unit of information. Bits are transmitted in entire blocks rather than individually, depending upon the particular data communications application. We'll explain why in this chapter.

Bit Rate is used as a measurement of transmission speed expressed in bits per second (bps). For instance, data is commonly transmitted at 300, 1200, 2400, 4800 and 9600 bps. Higher speeds like 14,400 bps and 1,500,000 bps are often abbreviated as 14.4 Kbps and 1.5 Mbps.

Baud Rate is often confused with bit rate. It is actually the number of signal transitions per period of time on the phone line. The baud rate and bit rate are typically the same at 300 bps (300 bps equals 300 baud). The baud rate, however, can't exceed 2400 baud or approximately the bandwidth of the phone line. And yet we can transmit above 2400 bps. This is accomplished by coding or increasing the number of bits per baud. Thus, we transmit 4800 bps at 2400 baud (encoding two bits per baud), 9600 bps at 2400 baud (four bits per baud), etc.

Baseband describes one of two transmission techniques widely used in local area networks in which narrow bandwidth lines carry analog signals, one at a time.

Broadband describes the second transmission technique used in local networks where a cable bandwidth, wider than that used in baseband transmission, carries many signals at once, including data, audio and video. But more on these two types later.

Babel, as in Tower of. We used this in the introduction as an illustration to describe how equipment in data communications networks can be incompatible. For DTEs to communicate effectively, they must first use a common language called a transmission code.

TRANSMISSION CODES

Transmission codes can be described as a system of symbols and rules for representing data. The code must be common to both sending and receiving DTEs and should use a minimum of bits to transmit maximum data. The particular code used is usually determined by what the host is designed to recognize.

There are several codes currently used. Codes are characterized by "levels" as determined by the number of bits needed to represent a character. The number of levels also indicate the number of different characters that code can represent.

Transmission codes are "transparent" to the user. That is, which code is used to transmit data is not apparent to the user. So the letter "A" transmitted looks like the letter "A" received no matter what code is operating within the DTE.

Below are the more common codes used in data communications. Your primary concern with transmission codes is that all your equipment uses the same code.

Baudot is one of the oldest codes, used more widely in foreign countries than in the U.S. It is a 5-1evel code capable of generating 58 different characters. Its main application is with Teletype™ terminals and other telegraphic equipment.

One thing to note is that there is no error-checking capability with Baudot or no way of ensuring that the transmitted data arrives without errors.

EBCDIC is the Extended Binary Coded Decimal Interchange Code developed by IBM, and all IBM mainframes use it. EBCDIC was one of the first attempts to standardize transmission codes. Characters are represented as 8-bit structures, and the code has the capability of generating 256 characters.

ASCII stands for the American Standard Code for Information Interchange and is the transmission code commonly used by minicomputers and PCs, especially in the U.S.

Developed by ISO, the International Standards Organization, ASCII represents one of the most successful attempts at code standardization and is considered a standard for universal data transmission. As a 7-level code, it can generate 128 different characters. An eighth bit can be used for parity.

PARITY

We've mentioned parity without explaining what it is and why it poses such an important consideration. We'll answer one question with another: How do you know the data was received exactly as it was transmitted?

Line disturbances come with the territory. So if you run your data over phone lines, you also run the risk of changing a bit here and there due to problems like electrical energy in the air and ambient noise on the line. We'll discuss line distortion in Chapter 4, but those pops and crackles you sometimes hear during phone conversations can knock out more than a bit of information when you're transmitting high-speed data.

Among the solutions for transmission errors is a type of error-checking called parity. It's a technique for adding one or more bits to the data in order to make the "one" bits of each character add up to either an odd or even number. Thus, there are two kinds of parity, odd and even.

Parity can be further divided into vertical and horizontal parity. Vertical parity is a character parity system that is not as effective as horizontal parity but is less expensive. It's used primarily with asynchronous terminals.

In **vertical parity**, individual bits and bit placement are not checked. All the system is designed to do is count the "one" bits in each character and approve each character of transmitted data as error-free if the bits add up to an odd or even number as predetermined. If a bit is changed in transmission (a "one" bit becomes a "zero" or vice versa), the count is thrown off and the incorrect data is spotted (figure 3-1). But if an even number of bits are destroyed, then the bits will still add up to the expected odd or even number and inaccurate data goes undetected.

An improvement on vertical parity is **horizontal parity**, also known as LRC or **Longitudinal Redundancy Check**. LRC looks at all the bits of a block of data as opposed to vertical parity, which only looks at a character. The most effective LRC is CRC or **Cyclic**

Here's an example of even vertical parity. To make the one bits add up to an even number, the parity bit is either a one or a zero. If a data bit is reversed in transmission (as indicated by the dotted numbers), the one bits will add up to an odd number and the bad data is detected, as with byte C. If two bits are reversed, though, the bad data goes undetected, as with byte D.

figure 3-1

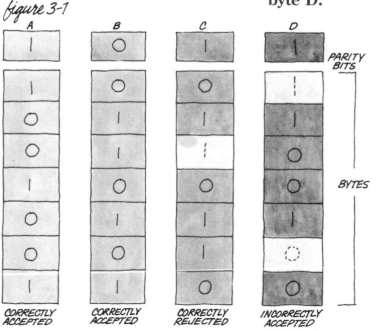

A	B	C	D

A — CORRECTLY ACCEPTED
B — CORRECTLY ACCEPTED
C — CORRECTLY REJECTED
D — INCORRECTLY ACCEPTED

PARITY BITS

BYTES

Redundancy Check. These error-checking techniques are used primarily with synchronous terminals in the transmission of entire blocks of data. CRC usually generates two bytes called block check characters which are added to each block. These **block check characters** detect bad data using a statistical method to check the accuracy of every bit in every character of the entire block of transmitted data.

PROTOCOLS

As we mentioned in Chapter 1, protocols are a set of methods or procedures that govern the transmission of data between DTEs. They're the rules of the road that make communication work, ensuring that the data sent is the data received.

To fully understand the importance of protocols, let's look at the relationship between protocols and transmission codes.

Transmission codes are the language the data is transformed into. Protocols govern the transfer of that data. Again, both are transparent to the user in the same way you're not aware of how someone is assembling their thoughts while they're talking to you.

Taking this analogy further, if verbal language and transmission codes are similar, what are the steps involved in speaking with someone? First you get the person's attention, he then acknowledges that he's listening, you speak, and hopefully he nods that he's understood you. If we compare this to a data transmission, all except the actual spoken message can be called protocol.

For data to be transmitted between DTEs, the following steps must be considered:

---

1. Does the receiving DTE know I want to transmit?
2. Is it ready to receive the data?
3. Was the data received without errors?
4. If errors were found, which data should be retransmitted?

The answers to these elementary questions are encoded and framed around your data every time you transmit to another DTE, in the form of protocols.

TRANSMISSION METHODS AND COMMON PROTOCOLS

Asynchronous transmission, also known as "start/stop" transmission, was mentioned briefly in Chapter Two. This is one of two techniques used to ensure that the receiving DTE begins reading the transmitted data at the correct character. If data is transmitted as a series of zeros and ones, the receiving DTE must be able to recognize when to start sampling the data or the data will be read incorrectly. This is accomplished with start and stop bits as illustrated in figure 3-2.

Characters are input and transmitted in the same random fashion that the operator keys in the data. Within the transmitting DTE, start and stop bits are attached to every character telling the receiving DTE when to start and stop sampling the data. So synchronization is continually re-established every time a start bit is detected.

Asynchronous transmission is most often used with slower, "dumb" terminals. The advantages are that it allows for variable speed

Asynchronous transmission uses "start" and "stop" bits around each character so that the receiving DTE will recognize when to start sampling the data.

figure 3-2

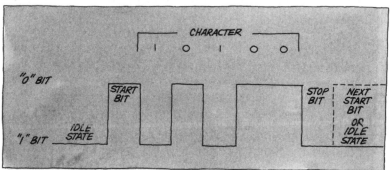

transmissions and regains synchronization quickly. Plus, asynchronous operation can be a less expensive form of transmission since it requires less sophisticated equipment.

This type of transmission is somewhat ineffi-cient, however, because start/stop bits plus idle time between characters slow down the data throughput rate. And since asynchronous terminals are usually unbuffered, there's no automatic retransmission-on-error (unless multiplexers are used). Data must be rekeyed until it's received correctly.

Unlike asynchronous transmission, **syn-chronous** transmission uses sophisticated modems to recover "clock" signals from the data on the phone line. The modems use the clock signals to synchronize the receiving DTE with the transmitting DTE. With asyn-chronous transmission, the DTEs are synchronized only on a character by character basis and are not syn-chronized otherwise.

Rather than transmitting individual characters framed by start/stop bits, entire blocks of data are rou-tinely transmitted from the terminal's buffer. Block size is determined by buffer size and phone circuit charac-teristics. Shorter blocks are more efficient to transmit in the presence of errors because retransmission is faster. But larger blocks are more efficient to transmit in the absence of errors because more data is received with less overhead and you're not waiting as often for an acknowledgment.

So how is data synchronization accomplished? Figure 3-3 shows how a transmitted block of data is constructed. (In this example, the block of data—or frame—is in an IBM protocol called SDLC, which we'll look at shortly.) Note that the frame is divided into a header area, a user area, and a trailer area. The header and trailer are further subdivided into fields (flag, address, control, frame check sequence, flag). Each of these fields contains a bit pattern that is generated by the sender of the frame and read by the receiver of the

frame in order to perform functions such as error control. The flags signal the beginning and end of a block
of data.

Because of additional features like sophisticated
clocking circuitry, synchronous transmission is a more
expensive way to transmit your data. But aside from
equipment costs, there are several advantages, such as
nearly error-free data transmission, enhanced throughput, and reduced line costs resulting from higher transmission speeds. Below we've listed some of the most
common synchronous protocols.

SDLC. Synchronous Data Link Control, a full-
or half-duplex bit-oriented protocol, has replaced 3270
BISYNC (Binary Synchronous Communication Protocol) as the most commonly used synchronous protocol.
It is used by IBM in its Systems Network Architecture
(SNA) networks. BISYNC was developed by IBM in the
mid-1960s and is to be found where older DTEs are still
in use. It is a half-duplex, character-oriented protocol
most often used in polled environments.

HDLC. High-level Data Link Control is the
CCITT international standard. (For more on the
CCITT, see Chapter 5.) It is bit-oriented rather than character-oriented
like BISYNC. HDLC operates over a
wider range of network environments
as well as over full-duplex lines,
thereby reducing transmission time.

A transmitted block of synchronous data, such as this SDLC frame, is divided into three major areas.

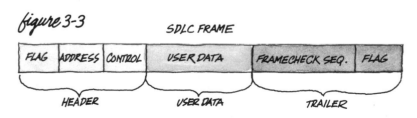

figure 3-3

SDLC FRAME

| FLAG | ADDRESS | CONTROL | USER DATA | FRAMECHECK SEQ. | FLAG |

HEADER   USER DATA   TRAILER

29

So now you understand everything you need to know about how data is passed back and forth between DTEs. The adrenalin is racng through your body like a greased parity bit, and your wife, husband or loved one just bought you a very expensive synchronous terminal with matching modems.

When that block of data goes streaking out of your buffer (remember, synchronous terminals are buffered), does it really have to share the same phone line with conversations about the latest soap or how Ricky bit the dog? Or do you have a choice which line your data travels over and the company it keeps?

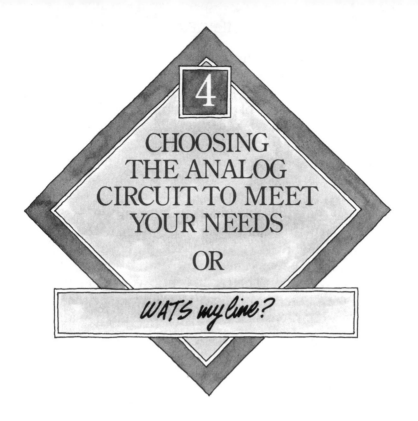

4

CHOOSING THE ANALOG CIRCUIT TO MEET YOUR NEEDS

OR

WATS my line?

This may sound a little simplistic but it's true—choosing a medium for transporting your data is like buying tires for your car. Anything that holds air will get you on the road. But whether you arrive looking the same as when you left will depend on how carefully you matched the characteristics of the tires to the requirements of your car and your driving habits.

Selecting a transmission speed is a function of the terminal, the modems that drive the data along the line, and the quality of the line itself. Transmission lines, also known as circuits, are simply vehicles or media for transporting your data.

The first way of choosing a type of line is in terms of speed and bandwidth. The general rule is, the wider the bandwidth, the faster the transmission rate. Increasing the speed of transmission beyond what the line can handle will only boost the amount of bad data received at the other end.

In reality, you could transmit your data over any number of media including wire, coaxial cable, microwave and satellite. Except for satellite because of the time delay, you would never know by what medium your data was transported. In other words, if you transmitted over voice-grade coaxial and voice-grade microwave, the characteristics of the "line" are the same in terms of speed, distortion, and error rate.

The two types of lines used to carry data are called leased and dial.

Leased lines, also known as private lines, are obtained from a common carrier like the phone company. In general, they are four-wire, full-duplex, which eliminates turnaround time for increased transmission speeds. The leased line is a permanent connection for a particular subscriber, providing end-to-end connectivity between a terminal and a device at the other end of the line.

Conditioning will be discussed later in this chapter but briefly, it is the process of reducing line distortion. Because we're dealing with the same line for all transmissions, lines can be conditioned to reduce line problems. This, in addition to no turnaround time, gives leased lines the capability to carry high volumes of data at high speeds with low error rates.

With leased lines, transmission can occur between separate facilities within a city or between different geographic locations entirely. Leased lines become economical only if you use them enough to justify the flat monthly rate. This means frequent transmissions of short duration like bank transactions or less frequent, longer transmissions such as file transfers.

Dial, switched or public lines (all names for the same thing), carry the bulk of data communications. This is the most wide reaching network—the same one you make your own phone calls on. So you can route your data to anyone or anything with access to the telephone network. All you do is dial the phone number of the receiving DTE's modem.

Dial lines have several other advantages. Because you can dial any data communications equipment that has its own phone number, one terminal serves many functions. And you're charged only for the particular transmission just like a regular phone call (though the rate structure is different). In fact, the cost can often be absorbed by your company's own WATS or tie-line service.

In terms of disadvantages, historically, dial modems were two-wire, half-duplex and this would often result in long turnaround times. However, the trend today is moving more and more in favor of two-wire, full-duplex dial transmission for medium- to high-speed requirements, eliminating the delay associated with half-duplex dial transmission.

In fact, 2400 bps full-duplex dial modems have become standard in the marketplace, with features like auto-call and auto-answer for more flexible use. And applying new technologies, dial modems are available at speeds of 4800, 9600, and now 14,400 bps with many of the advanced features traditionally found only in leased line modems, providing very high data reliability. In fact, when selected with additional options, high speed dial modems are able to handle many leased line modem applications. More on this in the next chapter. (This is becoming a real page turner.)

But still, dial lines are inherently slower than leased lines. One reason is that usable bandwidth is reduced because of certain characteristics common to dial lines. Remember, the narrower the bandwidth, the slower the transmission rate. Another factor is analog line noise. Switching gear at the phone company's central offices creates additional line noise contributing to data errors. And because there's no way of knowing which line your data will be routed over, dial lines cannot be conditioned by the telephone company to lower error rates and increase speeds.

Another problem encountered in dial transmission is that when transmitting more than 1,000 miles via dial lines, there's a high probability of going over satellite facilities, which greatly lengthens response time. But if you're not a user who needs to transmit high volumes of data at very high speeds across the country, using dial lines can be very cost-effective. This is why dial lines are most often used for time sharing applications which generally don't involve long, frequent transmissions.

Though the laws of physics regarding dial transmission can't change, the technology has, making great strides despite the constraints to assure better and better transmission quality. For instance, dial modem technology now features automatic error detection and error correction capabilities. These features identify garbled data resulting from line disturbances and indicate an error has been received. Many dial modems then retransmit the data until it's received correctly.

In **Dual Dial** communications, two phone calls are made from the same location to establish two dial connections between high speed modems. Since each direction of traffic has its own pair of wires, data can be transmitted full-duplex at speeds of 9600 bps and sometimes even higher. This procedure, also known as **dial backup**, is typically used to restore service temporarily in the event of a leased line failure.

ANALOG LINE DISTORTION

There's more in the telephone line than your data. Perhaps it's old data that never got to where it was going. The fact is, when you transmit over a noisy line, your data can arrive looking like Swiss cheese.

Actually, if data communications has enemies, it's line noise, transmission speed, and plain old physics. Here's the story. Every circuit has resistance, inductance, and capacitance (commonly known as impedance), so the signal naturally becomes distorted as it travels the line. Two kinds of distortion affecting the signal are **frequency response**, which is a variation in signal strength for different frequency tones, and **envelope delay,** where some frequencies are delayed more than others. That is, tones of different frequencies, transmitted simultaneously will be received at different times.

The problem here is that high speed data transmission requires good frequency response and reduced envelope delay. Plus, there are line impairments like random or thermal noise caused by molecular vibration within electronic circuitry, static from the atmosphere, interference from electrical equipment like fluorescent lights and even noise on the line generated from the phone company's own equipment.

And if this isn't enough to bludgeon your data until it's unrecognizable, figure 4-1 describes more line demons. Line hits are the primary source of error in low- and medium-speed transmission and may destroy the data in transmission for the duration of the hit. So what do you do? A solution for some of these problems is conditioning.

ANALOG LEASED LINE CONDITIONING
The objective of conditioning is to have your data arrive looking the way it left. By improving overall frequency response of the line, you can ultimately transmit data at higher speeds. But remember, dial lines can't be conditioned because you're dialing up over a different line each time you transmit data. There's no way of knowing which line to condition. So only private leased lines can be conditioned. Conditioning will never get you an absolutely "clean" line, but the distortion will be kept within prescribed limits.

Modems of 2400 bps and faster have built-in equalizers to help improve transmission over any kind of line. These equalizers are especially necessary for dial lines where there are no other means of conditioning the circuit. Equalization in high-speed modems will be discussed further in Chapter 5.

The telephone company is responsible for adding conditioning equipment to your leased line (at your request) and the charge is figured into your monthly fee. Equalizers help compensate for frequency response problems and envelope delay while amplifiers allow you to adjust your overall signal to the correct level.

As a user, you can purchase two additional services from the telephone company to improve the quality even further. The first is type C conditioning, which is divided into five categories, C1 through C5. The most commonly used are C1, C2, and C4, which improve amplitude and delay characteristics of the line.

LINE DEMONS
figure 4-1

- [ ] **Phase Jitter** is the shifting of phase of one part of the frequency tone relative to an earlier part of the tone.
- [ ] **Harmonic Distortion** is an additional signal generated by the nonlinear characteristics of the transmission line which distorts the primary signal.
- [ ] **Frequency Shift** means the frequency tone that's received is different from the tone sent.
- [ ] **Line Hits** are momentary electrical disturbances on the line caused by atmospheric conditions, telephone company switching equipment, and radio/microwave transmission. These include:
  Dropouts—sudden large reductions in a signal level that last more than several milliseconds.
  Phase Hits—sudden uncontrolled changes in phase of the received signal.
  Gain Hits—sudden uncontrolled increases or decreases in the received signal level.
  Impulse Noise—sudden "bursts" of noise of very short duration.

The second service is type D, which specifies limits on signal-to-noise and harmonic distortions. Type D is divided into several categories, differentiated by specification parameters and price. That's not to say that the most expensive type is the best. It all depends on your application. However, you cannot combine two types of C conditioning or two types of D conditioning. But you can choose one type from group C and one type from group D to do the job.

The phone company keeps impulse noise, frequency shift, and phase jitter within certain guidelines. Phase hits, gain hits, and dropouts are not controlled at present, though they can be monitored by network control equipment so that the user is warned before there's a serious problem. This is described in more detail in Chapter 11.

If it makes you feel any better, almost none of the line distortion we've discussed is even perceptible to the human ear, though it's happening throughout your phone conversations. Unfortunately, to your data communications equipment connected via unconditioned lines, if the line isn't clean, it's like trying to talk on the phone while jets are landing. Conditioning and equalization are generally very effective and make data transmission possible at speeds once thought unattainable.

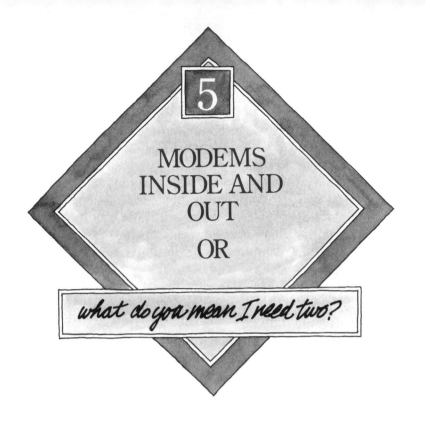

5

MODEMS
INSIDE AND
OUT

OR

what do you mean I need two?

Let's suppose you've got a terminal that you want to connect to a host computer via, say, a dial phone line. Can you transmit digital information directly across the phone line?

No. (If the word "maybe" even crossed your mind, go immediately back to Chapter 1 and reread aloud.) Of course you need modems, one at either end. And how is the connection facilitated between the modems (DCE equipment) and the terminal and host computer (DTE equipment) at either end? By a common interface. A what?

INTERFACES

Very simply, an interface is an electrical connection between DCE and DTE equipment. The connection method is defined by the distance between equipment, the amount of time your terminal and host are communicating, and by the particular interface available with certain DTE devices. The main thing to remember is that when selecting data communications equipment, the DCE and DTE equipment must have compatible interfaces or you literally can't connect them (a new twist in the "Tower of Babel" theme).

There are three types of interfaces—voltage, contact closure, and current loop. All we're really concerned with here are voltage interfaces. And most equipment

EIA 232-D uses a 25-pin connector where each pin is assigned a particular circuit-controlling function. Interfaces like EIA 232-D allow different brands of equipment to be "plug-compatible."

using voltage interfaces conforms to the Electronic Industries Association (**EIA**) standard **EIA 232-D** (the upgraded version of the EIA's old RS 232-C standard). You might recall we mentioned this interface in Chapter 1. The reason for a standard is for the sake of compatibility between different brands of equipment.

figure 5-1

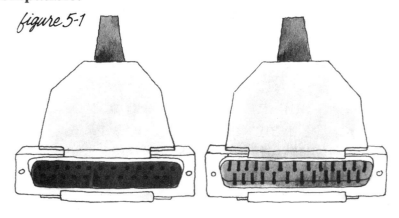

EIA 232-D uses a 25-pin connector or plug where each pin is assigned a particular circuit-controlling function (figure 5-1). Such functions as timing signals, used to synchronize synchronous transmissions, operate through specific pins. The DTE equipment generally has the male connector and the DCE equipment has the female connector.

EIA 232-D is specified for up to 19,200 bps whether you're transmitting synchronously or asynchronously. A direct digital link of no greater than 50 feet is specified by this interface regardless of the transmission rate, but EIA 232-D can be used effectively with direct digital links of several hundred feet at slower data rates using specially shielded cables.

An important consideration if you anticipate doing business internationally is whether EIA 232-D is also a standard outside the U.S. The answer is "yes" and "no." The Comité Consultatif International de Télégraphie et Téléphonie (Consultative Committee for International Telegraphy and Telephony or **CCITT**) is the EIA's counterpart in other countries and also sets standards for equipment compatibility. The CCITT has developed a functionally compatible interface identical to EIA 232-D called **V.24/V.28**. This allows data communications equipment to be plug-compatible worldwide.

The U.S. government has never really supported EIA 232-D and has instead been promoting a standard called **EIA 530**, which also covers both synchronous and asynchronous transmission. Like EIA 232-D, EIA 530 describes the functional and mechanical characteristics of an interface. EIA 530 uses a 25-pin connector so it can accommodate circuit controlling functions.

An advantage of EIA 530 is that it allows for longer direct digital connections between DTEs of up to 2,000 feet, it will support transmission speeds up to 2 Mbps, and it reduces crosstalk (not quite the same as cursing; this is where one wire's signals interfere with another's). EIA 530 is steadily gaining in popularity.

HANDSHAKING

The steps involved in "handshaking" will remind you of our discussion of protocols in Chapter 3. It is a procedure where control signals are exchanged between modems when DTE equipment at one end of a line attempts to transmit to DTE equipment at the other end.

Handshaking amounts to a DTE gaining the attention of its modem in order to make sure that it's okay to start transmitting data.

The transmitting modem functions as the social director making the introductions throughout the network. This includes announcing that one DTE would like to transmit, and ensuring that the modems will be synchronized for data transmission. The signals exchanged are predetermined by the particular device and circuit standards.

Figure 5-2 lists the sequence of these signals and describes what they mean.

This is the basic sequence of modem control signals used to establish a dial line connection between the DTE and the modem.

figure 5-2

MODEM CONTROL SIGNAL	FUNCTION
Ring indicator	Set by modem when telephone rings
Data terminal ready	Set by device to enable modem to answer an incoming call on a dial line. Reset by device to disconnect call
Data set ready	Set by modem when it is powered on and not in test mode, and in response to data terminal ready and ring indicator
Request to send	Set by device when user program wishes to transmit
Carrier detect	Set by modem when signal is present
Clear to send	Set by modem when transmission may begin
Transmit data	Data sent from device to modem
Receive data	Data received by device

TURNAROUND TIME

There are modems that support half-duplex operation, which means they alternate between transmitting and receiving data over two-wire lines. And then there are modems that run full-duplex, transmitting and receiving simultaneously over four-wire circuits (and some over two-wire as we've explained).

There are three components of **turnaround time** that can slow down your application. The first is the time required for a modem to switch from receiving to transmitting data and vice versa. As you may have guessed, this delay is critical in half-duplex, two-wire operation. Running full-duplex allows the modems to establish "carrier," which keeps the communications link open in both directions at the same time. This way, both modems' transmitters can stay up and synchronized, eliminating turnaround time.

The second component of turnaround time is the error control procedure in synchronous data transmission governed by protocol. With older "stop and wait" protocols, every time a block of data is transmitted, there's a delay from the time the last character of the block is transmitted until an acknowledgement is received.

The third component of turnaround time is the delay that's inherent in certain transmission media. Using satellite transmission, for example, there's nearly a quarter second delay introduced in either direction.

TYPES OF MODEMS

Unlike terminals, modem classifications are more standardized and a little easier to follow. Modems are classified by the line facility they use to transmit data, the mode of transmission, and the applications they support.

The facilities used for data transmissions were covered in our discussion about bandwidth in Chapter 4. Modems can be divided into four line servicing groups: narrowband, voice-grade, wideband, and limited distance modems.

We'll discuss all four groups but, more than likely, voice-grade and/or limited distance modems would be the most appropriate for your network.

Narrowband modems are used in asynchronous transmission over four-wire lines at a top speed of 300 bps. These modems are used with teletype and other low-speed terminals.

Voice-grade modems can be divided into low-speed modems transmitting up to 1200 bps, medium-speed modems which transmit up to 4800 bps, and high-speed modems which support 9600 bps and above. Typical speeds are 300, 1200, 2400, 4800, 9600, 14,400, 16,800, and 19,200 bps.

The wider the bandwidth, the faster the transmission speed possible—which explains why wideband transmission is so fast. But the focus of technology has been on achieving higher data rates over voice-grade lines because they're accessible and economical to use. As a result of research and development supported by independent manufacturers, we're now able to transmit 16,800 bps and faster over the narrow 3,300 Hz bandwidth of the phone lines.

Wideband is used to carry computer-to-computer and other high-speed transmissions. A wideband group facility is usually a single channel that takes up the same bandwidth of 12 voice-grade circuits. The modems serving these lines handle speeds from 19.2 Kbps to 64 Kbps. Keep in mind, though, that you would need to be transmitting tremendous amounts of data to justify the expense of operating such a network.

Limited Distance Modems (LDMs), also known as short-haul modems, can be used in asynchronous or synchronous applications. Their transmission range is one to twenty miles at speeds of up to 1.5 Mbps. These modems require metallic lines and are most often used to transmit data within company facilities.

Limited distance modems are especially cost-effective at higher speeds as they're less expensive than either voice-grade or wideband modems.

ASYNCHRONOUS AND SYNCHRONOUS MODEMS

Again, we have to precede this section with the phrase "in general," because modem manufacturers are continually expanding the functionality and applications of new devices. This makes it difficult to neatly categorize the various modems available.

But, "in general," synchronous operation is more efficient, faster, and more expensive than asynchronous operation. Therefore high-speed modems are synchronous, and low-speed modems are asynchronous.

Asynchronous voice-grade modems typically have an upper limit of about 2400 bps and most commonly operate at around 1200 bps. However, modems that fall in the low end of the medium-speed voice-grade range (between 1200 bps and 2400 bps) may be designed to handle both asynchronous and synchronous transmission. For high-speed asynchronous applications, many modems have an asynchronous-to-synchronous converter option, which permits asynchronous data to be transmitted via synchronous modems.

ACOUSTIC COUPLERS

One of the earliest types of modems developed and still in use today is called an acoustic coupler. Rather than hardwired directly into a dial phone line, an acoustic coupler has built-in rubber cups that fit a standard telephone handset. After dialing the phone number of the device you want to transmit to, the communication link is made by placing the handset in the coupler to form an acoustic connection (rather than an electrical one) between the modem and the phone line.

The decision to develop a device that used a microphone and speaker was based on the telephone company's concern at the time that hard-wiring a device directly into a phone line could somehow damage their equipment. An acoustic coupler seemed like the safest alternative.

Acoustic couplers are asynchronous, low-speed devices usually compatible with low-speed Bell modems. We now have more advanced low-speed dial modems that plug directly into the phone jack, and the phone, in turn, plugs into the modem for a more reliable direct connection.

BELL-COMPATIBLE MODEMS

Bell-designed low-speed modems have been the accepted low-end standard in the U.S. for many years. Even though that standard is rapidly changing over to higher speed full-duplex transmission, these types of modems are still in use everywhere. While some independent manufacturers focus on high-speed technology, many of them also produce low-speed modems compatible with, and often exceeding, Bell standards. Some have even reduced entire Bell modems to a single printed circuit board known as a "card," or even to a single integrated circuit chip for more efficient use of space.

A few independent manufacturers produce Bell-compatible equipment that meets CCITT recommendations so it may be used outside the U.S. or used to communicate with DTE equipment in foreign countries. With a few exceptions most of Bell's equipment is not CCITT-compatible.

The following is a list of the most common low-end Bell modems.

The 103/113 is the lowest speed voice-grade modem with a data rate of up to 300 bps. It actually has two channels within the assigned bandwidth. One modem called the **originate** transmits on the first channel and receives on the second, while the other **answer** modem operates in the reverse.

In this way, two 103s can transmit to one another at the same time and not compete for the same channel. The 113A is originate only, the 113B is answer only and the 103 can change bands to act as either.

The 201C supports half-duplex synchronous transmission of 2400 bps over dial lines.

The 202S supports half-duplex operation of up to 1200 bps over dial lines. The 202T supports half-duplex dial transmission or full-duplex leased line transmission of up to 1800 bps. The 202T, however, requires a conditioned line to transmit faster than 1200 bps over leased lines.

The 208A operates half- or full-duplex over leased lines at 4800 bps. The 208B transmits at 4800 bps over dial lines but only in half-duplex.

The 212A is an asynchronous or synchronous, two-speed, full-duplex modem for dial lines. It uses 103 technology for asynchronous transmission at 300 bps and will operate either synchronously or asynchronously at 1200 bps.

CCITT-COMPATIBLE MODEMS

Few Bell modems are CCITT-compatible, but many independent manufacturers produce modems that are. The following are some of the most common dial and leased line CCITT-compatible modems and error correction schemes. You'd think all modems meeting CCITT requirements for a particular standard would be compatible. Unfortunately, not so. The problem lies in options in the CCITT recommendations that are open to interpretation.

V.22 bis is a 2400 bps point-to-point modem with fallback speeds of 300 and 1200 bps. Transmission is synchronous or asynchronous, full-duplex over two-wire, leased or dial lines.

V.27 is a 4800 bps point-to-point or multipoint modem with a fallback speed of 2400 bps. Transmission is synchronous, half-duplex over two-wire, and full-duplex over four-wire.

V.29 is a 9600 bps point-to-point or multipoint leased line modem with fallback speeds of 4800 and 2400 bps. Transmission is synchronous, half-duplex over two-wire, and full-duplex over four-wire.

V.32 is a 9600 point-to-point modem with a fallback speed of 4800 bps. Transmission is synchronous, full-duplex over two-wire, leased or dial lines. The error correction scheme specified by the CCITT for V.32 modems is V.42 (below).

47

V.32 bis extends V.32 to 14.4 Kbps. Today, high-speed dial is becoming increasingly popular for many applications. We'll look at an example in Chapter 12.

V.33 is a 14.4 Kbps point-to-point leased line modem similar to the V.32 with a fallback speed of 12 Kbps. Transmission is synchronous, half-duplex over two-wire and full-duplex over four-wire.

ERROR CORRECTION

Trellis Coded Modulation (TCM) is a forward error correction scheme used with high speed, synchronous leased line modems or with V.32 dial modems. It is designed to provide reliable data transmissions even over dial lines with poor quality. This scheme compares redundantly transmitted data and rejects distorted bits.

MNP™ (Microcom Networking Protocol) is a full-duplex error correction protocol that, because of its wide use, has become a de facto standard. In its favor is its ability to support five of the seven OSI layers. MNP is divided into classes 1 through 9. MNP 3 is used with 2400 bps modems and offers eight percent more throughput by removing the start and stop bits. MNP 5 and 6 are used with 9600 bps modems and, using data compression, double throughput. MNP 7 and 9 are used with higher speed modems.

LAPD (Link Access Protocol D) is a member of the HDLC family and the major competitor of MNP. Though it is already supported by many DTE manufacturers, we'll have to wait to see which technology emerges as the leader.

V.42 provides standardized error control in modems via either MNP Level 4 or LAPM protocol.

V.42 bis provides CCITT-standardized data compression.

MODULATION

We're going to view modems now from a different perspective—from the inside looking out.

In order to investigate and select the modem to meet your needs, you'll need to know a little bit about how they operate. This section does not require a course in electrical engineering—if you can plug in a toaster oven, you're all set.

The basic components of a modem are a transmitter, receiver, and power supply. The transmitter includes circuitry for, among other things, modulation.

As you know, there are two kinds of electricity: the battery kind which is direct current and the toaster oven kind which is alternating current. The phone lines also use alternating current, which characteristically grows and diminishes similar to a wave. When converted into an analog signal, data resembles this continuous wave form called a "sine wave".

A pure sine wave carries no information. But there are three parts of a sine wave that can be manipulated or modulated by the modem to represent data: frequency, amplitude, and phase. Modulation techniques have been developed around each of these three components.

The higher the modem speed, the more complex the modulation scheme needed to impress information on the sine wave. This of course means more complex circuitry contributing to overall cost. Briefly, here are the modulation techniques.

Frequency modulation, also known as Frequency Shift-Key modulation, is used for low-speed, asynchronous transmission. The number of waves per unit of space or frequency is varied while the height or amplitude of the waves is kept constant. So as seen in figure 5-3, a one bit is represented by two waves and a zero bit by four waves. FSK is limited to low-speed transmission because it's only capable of transmitting one bit per baud.

Four modulation techniques used to impress information on the sine wave. Higher speed modems require the more complex modulation schemes.

Amplitude modulation varies the height or amplitude of the waves while keeping the frequency constant. In figure 5-4, the waves representing the one bit are taller than the waves representing the zero bit. This modulation technique is often used to transmit data between 300 bps and 1200 bps. Amplitude modulation, like FSK,

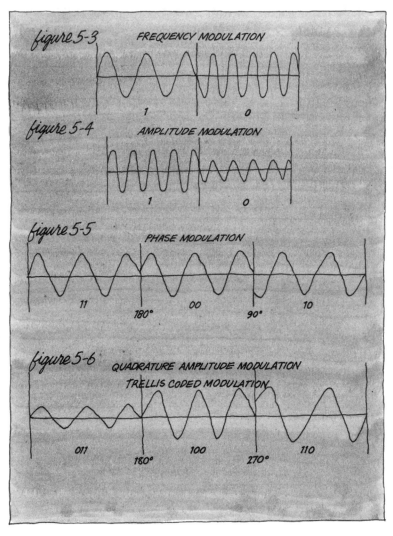

cannot transmit more than one bit per baud. And it's generally used in combination with other modulation techniques.

Phase modulation, also known as Phase Shift modulation, is one of the most difficult techniques to understand. If a normal sine wave is used to represent a one bit, then that wave shifted 180° out of phase is used to represent a zero bit. As illustrated in figure 5-5, a 180° shift in phase is actually the mirror image of the original wave. Phase modulation is most common in modems transmitting at 2400 bps and can transmit up to three bits per baud.

Quadrature amplitude modulation or QAM combines amplitude and phase modulation to achieve data rates of 4800 bps, 9600 bps and higher. Combining different amplitude signals and phase shifts makes it possible to modulate from four to seven bits per baud while keeping the baud rate within the 3300 Hz bandwidth limitations of the phone line. Figure 5-6 illustrates data transmitted via QAM.

A while ago, we mentioned **Trellis Coded Modulation** for high-speed transmission. TCM uses the same modulation scheme as QAM but with one very important difference. TCM provides error correction by adding on coded information to the transmitted sequence of signals. The result is high quality performance at speeds from 9600 bps to 19.2 Kbps. Figure 5-6 shows the frequency scheme for TCM after the encoding process. Notice that it looks just like QAM.

EQUALIZATION

Equalization circuitry built into the modem compensates for frequency response and envelope delay to permit higher transmission rates and becomes more complex the higher the speed.

Manual equalizers are used in lower speed modems and limited distance transmission products. These equalizers are manually set to compensate for average line conditions, which include frequency response and envelope delay.

Automatic adaptive equalizers are more
expensive to manufacture than fixed equalizers and are
used in modems operating at 2400 bps and faster over
dial or leased lines. The automatic adaptive equalizer
continually readjusts or adapts itself in order to compensate for changes in line quality. This is especially
useful in dial line operation where each new call presents different line conditions.

MODEM FEATURES AND OPTIONS
Modem features and options translate into greater
operational flexibility. But one manufacturer's features
are another manufacturer's options. It's important to
understand from the vendor what features are factory
installed and what enhancements may be added on
later. The following is only a partial list of what's available in the industry.

Multiport capability is similar to a basic multiplexer where a few communication lines can be handled by a single modem.

Multiple speed selection permits you to continue transmitting, even while the quality of the phone
line is degrading, by falling back to a lower transmission speed, thus reducing the error rate.

Dial backup allows you to switch from your
leased line to a dial line or lines in the event the private
line fails in some way.

Voice/data capability allows you to alternate
voice transmission with data transmission on the
same line.

Self-testing features or diagnostics are a way
of performing local and remote testing through the
modem to determine if there's a problem in either the
line or the modem.

Auto-call automatically places calls for a
modem on the dial network to eliminate operator
intervention.

Auto-answering automatically answers incoming calls to the modem.

A built-in **Adaptive Rate System (ARS)** allows a modem to continuously sense varying line conditions and adjust according to the highest possible speed.

Echo cancellation is an advanced technique that eliminates echoes and subsequent distortions for two-wire dial line transmission over short and long distances at speeds up to 9,600 bps.

Phase roll compensation is a modem feature that automatically adjusts for frequency differences between interexchange carriers (long-distance companies).

Modem substitution switch is an external option that allows you to reroute your data through a "hot" spare modem (which is already powered up) in the event the original modem fails.

Asynchronous to synchronous converter permits an asynchronous DTE to operate with a synchronous modem.

There are also **soft strapping options**, which are built into the modem and activated by the user for a variety of functions. Strapping options include switching from half- to full-duplex operation, or going from two- to four-wire transmission, or converting a point-to-point modem into a multipoint modem and vice versa.

SELECTING MODEMS

Three basic criteria in selecting modems are the **volume** of transmitted data and the **speed** and **distance** it needs to travel. Volume is a function of both the characters per transaction and the number of transactions per day required to support your application. Volume of traffic, then, not only determines the speed of transmission but whether you should use leased or dial lines. And distance helps determine whether you need limited distance modems or long-haul modems.

Here are some other questions to consider:

1. Will the modem interface be compatible with your DTEs?
2. Will the new modems be able to communicate with any existing ones?

3. Will the modem be used for leased or dial operation?
4. Will the modem be used in a point-to-point or multipoint configuration?
5. What kind of diagnostic capabilities do you need?
6. What kind of error rate can you accept?
7. What is the modem's mean time between failures (MTBF)?
8. Is there a multiple speed capability?
9. What is involved if you want to add modem options?
10. Do the modems have network control capability to keep your network running despite network problems?

Up until now, we've been talking about a terminal and host computer connected by a single phone line with two modems, or what's commonly called a point-to-point configuration.

Let's say you have a manufacturing business. Your order-entry department is linked to a distant host via a synchronous terminal and a pair of 2400 bps modems on a point-to-point leased line. Why synchronous equipment? Because order entry is a synchronous application. The terminal operator needs to be able to move the terminal's cursor from field to field and to fill out a different order form for each of your products, have it checked for accuracy, then send all that information to the host. And you've selected a leased line rather than a dial line because frequent transmissions make dial lines uneconomical.

Several months have gone by and your business has grown beyond all expectations. Now you have four people in your office who need to enter orders into the computer.

While people are idly waiting their turn to play musical chairs with the system, the information that needs to be transmitted is backing up. The data communications network that once was perfectly adequate is no longer getting the job done. What do you do?

a. Sell the business.
b. Rent storage to stockpile the information that is backing up.
c. Fire the next person who complains.
d. Somehow add more terminals and not go under with phone line costs.

The next chapter will explore only one of the above.

6

EXPANDING THE NETWORK: PART I

OR

getting the drop on the network

So three more people in your office need their own terminals to access the same application from the host computer (i.e., order entry). All of them will still transmit randomly and essentially simultaneously. But for the sake of convenience, rather than rotate four people at one terminal, you decide to add three more synchronous terminals and expand your data communications network. Now the question is, how do you connect these four terminals to the same host?

Let's say you're a firm believer in learning by trial and error and you have an unlimited budget to learn with. In your estimation, your business has reached a plateau (along with the economy), and your data communications needs won't be changing for quite a while. With this in mind, you add three more synchronous terminals, three more leased lines, and six more 2400 bps modems, as illustrated in figure 6-1. Everything appears to be working perfectly, right up until you get your first phone bill.

It's becoming obvious that as your network continues to grow, the time could come when your line and modem costs would easily outweigh the cost of your DTE equipment, including the host itself. The object now is to "reconnect the dots" or reconfigure your network in a way that makes the most efficient use of the communication lines.

One solution would be to reconfigure the network so all four terminals share the same line, since they're all transmitting to the same place. What you then have is a **multipoint** or multidrop network, as illustrated in figure 6-2.

Expanding your system from one point-to-point network to four point-to-point networks quadruples your communications expenses.

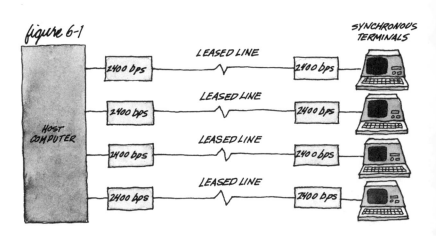

58

You already meet the requirements for multi-point operation. You're using leased rather than dial lines. And your terminals are synchronous, address-able, single application devices that operate at the same speed, use the same protocol, and transmit "similar" kinds of data (i.e., order-entry information). This allows all four terminals to share the same communication line and **computer port.**

In all our diagrams, we've drawn the host as a box with communications lines. Each line actually con-nects to the host via a port, and the rule is, only one line to a port. The host has a limited number of ports, so once they're filled you can't add more terminals to your network unless you buy additional computer ports (which is very expensive) or somehow can share ports with multiple terminals. For these reasons, and the fact that you're using only one leased line, a multipoint net-work is an economical alternative. **A multipoint net-work eliminates three leased lines and three modems.** But how do the four terminals com-pete for line time?

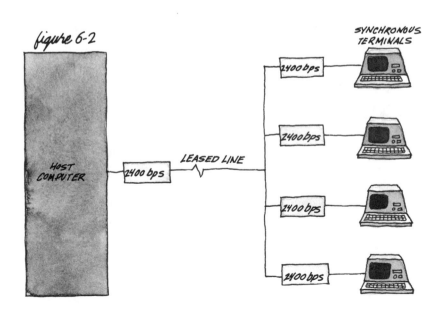

figure 6-2

They don't. Multipoint networks are by definition **polled**. Polling is accomplished, as we've discussed, by the host asking each terminal, in a predetermined order, if it has data to transmit. This is why terminals in a multipoint, polled network must be intelligent enough to be addressable; they also require buffers, since they can't transmit simultaneously. The polling is all handled by the host. It checks each terminal's buffer for requests, acknowledges those requests, and then searches its own application software for the answers.

MULTIPOINT MODEMS
One of the drawbacks of operating in a polled environment is that each terminal must wait its turn to transmit, which slows down communications. But for multipoint networks with greater throughput requirements, special higher speed modems have been designed to specifically reduce polling time. The key is to reduce a major component of turnaround time called **training time**.

Training time is only a factor in multipoint operation when the remote terminals want to transmit to the host. Each time transmission is initiated, the receiving modem at the host must **train** or adjust to the conditions of that particular line segment. These conditions include amplitude response, delay distortion, and timing recovery. In other words, all the information the receiving modem must have in order to recover the signal is **initialized** for each transmission.

This is accomplished by the transmitting modem sending a predetermined signal or "training sequence" down the line to the receiving modem. The receiving modem, knowing how the training sequence should appear, is able to recognize how specific line conditions have distorted the sequence, and make the necessary adjustments to its receiver. Thereafter, the modem's equalizer makes small adjustments to fine-tune and compensate for more subtle line changes.

This training process usually takes about nine milliseconds (ms) or less in a multipoint network. Nine ms hardly seems like much to worry about except when you consider the high number of trains required in a multipoint network. Long retrains can slow the polling process down considerably. The faster the host site modem can train, the less time the terminal has to wait to send its data.

What we've just described is a multipoint network where all the "drops" (i.e., terminals) are located in the same building. Now what if you want to do the same thing across a number of geographically dispersed offices, linking the offices to the host via one leased line. Schematically, both kinds of multipoint networks look the same. However, in each city where there's a terminal or drop, the telephone company, through its local central office, must set up the multipoint connection, providing an **analog bridge** to the line (figure 6-3). This analog bridge combines lines from several dispersed offices into one line to optimize the flow of data traffic back to the host computer.

We've drawn a geographically dispersed multipoint network in a slightly different way to emphasize the role of the telephone company. Each circle represents a telephone company central office where an analog bridge is implemented to connect that particular terminal to your leased line.

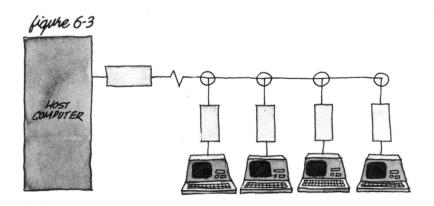

figure 6-3

HOST COMPUTER

What the telephone company is actually providing is a series of point-to-point segments and analog bridges to link up the multipoint network. Though this sounds like a complex process, it is still less expensive than paying for individual point-to-point lines between the host and each of your terminals.

Modems have been developed specifically for multipoint applications, where quick response at each location means greater throughput.

Asymmetrical multipoint modems offer higher outbound speeds. When implementing a multipoint network, the remote modem's training time is influenced by the inbound transmission speed. The higher the speed, the longer the training time. This is not an issue for the host site modem transmitting outbound data. And in fact, in most host applications, there's more traffic outbound than inbound. In response, asymmetrical multipoint modems were developed using TCM to transmit outbound at 14.4 Kbps, nearly doubling throughput, and inbound at 9600 bps, reducing training time.

The **multichannel multipoint modem** is designed to support two or more independent multipoint applications on a single multipoint line. The multiple applications are able to share the same circuit through a built-in multiplexing technique.

An important feature in multipoint modems is the ability to respond when line quality on only one or a few drops degrades. In the past, the entire multipoint network had to be slowed to the speed of the worst drop. Today, multipoint modems are available that can accept different inbound rates from remote modems to compensate for varying line quality, allowing unaffected drops to continue operating at maximum speed.

DIGITAL BRIDGE

Just as the telephone company provides analog bridging when terminals are not located within the same building, you can install a **digital bridge** (formerly known as a digital sharing device or DSD) to reduce costs when they are.

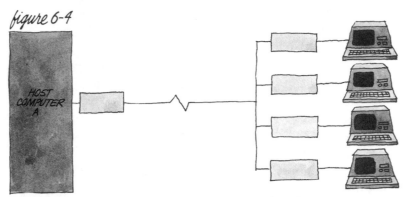

figure 6-4

This is a typical multipoint network where terminals are located in the same office.

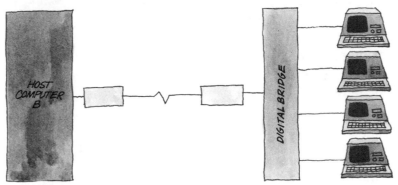

Is the same network, a digital bridge operating as a modem sharing unit eliminates three modems.

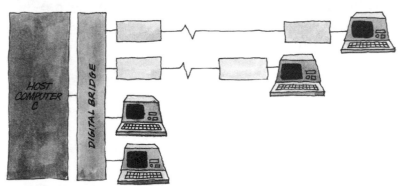

Here the digital bridge acts as a port sharing unit to funnel the transmissions from two remote DTEs and two host-site DTEs into the same computer port.

The digital bridge can be located near the remote terminals to reduce the number of modems needed. Or, it can also be located next to the host to reduce the number of ports required for a series of point-to-point lines. This multipurpose device saves money by enabling up to six modems or ports, in any combination, to share a single connection with one remote modem or port. The channels of the digital bridge can be set to accept either terminal (DTE) or modem (DCE) interfaces by pushing a button (figure 6-4).

The digital bridge handles either synchronous or asynchronous data (but not simultaneously). As a modem sharing unit, the digital bridge replaces all but one of the remote modems in a multipoint network where the terminals are **clustered** together. The digital bridge is also transparent to your network, so even your modems and terminals aren't aware the device is operating.

It's easy to imagine scenarios where going to multipoint operation would not be an appropriate solution, or at least not the primary one. Remember, all these multipoint applications we've been discussing require single application, synchronous terminals that use the same protocol and run at the same speed. What if your requirements change? What other ways could you cost-effectively expand your network?

7

EXPANDING THE NETWORK: PART II

OR

running a mux

Let's say the economy takes a sudden upward turn (this is hypothetical) and your business starts expanding. You don't need to add more terminals yet, but all four of your terminal operators insist they now need to transmit simultaneously and the polling network is too slow. Also, your operators are now more specialized in their job functions, and the data they're transmitting and accessing reflects this increased specialization.

You no longer meet the requirements of a polled multipoint network. What is the alternative to bearing the expense of four point-to-point leased lines?

MULTIPLEXED MODEMS

A simple economical solution is to replace your original 2400 bps modems with a pair of 9600 bps modems, each with its own built-in four-channel multiplexer. Your network now resembles figure 7-1. These four-channel modems will give you four 2400 bps channels combined into one 9600 bps line for synchronous transmission. The sum of the individual channels cannot exceed the total line speed. You'll also notice when looking at figure 7-1 that four channels require four computer ports. That's the trade-off when you choose to have your terminals transmit simultaneously.

Business continues to boom, *Fortune* magazine is considering you for the cover, and you've just opened up a district office. You assign one of your four terminal operators to the new office and tell him to take his terminal with him. This, of course, opens up a 2400 bps channel in the 9600 bps multiplexed modem located in your regional office.

In this situation, using two 9600 bps four-channel multiplexed modems eliminates eight 2400 bps modems and three phone lines.

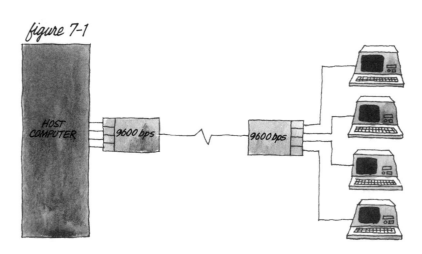

figure 7-1

You then purchase two 2400 bps modems. One connects to the 2400 bps channel vacated in your regional office (figure 7-2). The other 2400 bps modem hooks up to the terminal now located at the remote district office. The data now runs over the phone line to the regional office, goes through the pair of 9600 bps modems and back to the host. Your new expenses are two 2400 bps modems, a local phone line, and you just made what's called a **tail circuit** as illustrated in figure 7-2.

MULTIPLEXERS

If you wanted more than four terminals to be able to transmit simultaneously in a multipoint environment, and/or you wanted to mix synchronous and asynchronous terminals, and/or use different speed terminals, and you definitely wanted to continue to reduce line costs—you would next want to consider installing separate stand-alone multiplexers.

A tail circuit is created by remoting a terminal from the regional office and replacing it with a 2400 bps modem. The link between the 2400 bps modem and the 9600 bps multiplexed modem is a digital one.

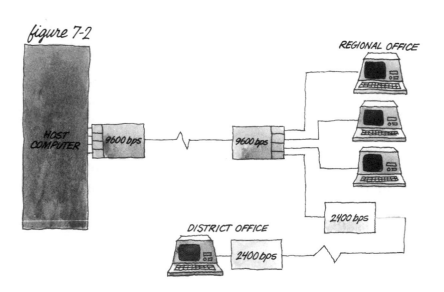

figure 7-2

REGIONAL OFFICE

HOST COMPUTER

9600 bps

9600 bps

DISTRICT OFFICE

2400 bps

2400 bps

As with modems, you need a pair of multiplexers—one to undo what the other one did, which in this case is called "demultiplexing."

Multiplexers, nicknamed "muxes" (contrary to popular belief, this is not even remotely a dirty word), work to combine several low- to medium-speed terminal transmissions onto one high speed voice-grade line running to the host. The second multiplexer demultiplexes the signal back into lower speed transmissions and routes each input to its own computer port.

Other than for the applications listed above, multiplexers are also used when phone lines connecting to the host are parallel for some distance. The longer the distance that the communication lines run parallel, the more money you save using multiplexers. Multiplexer technology has driven down transmission costs faster than line rates have gone up.

There are three kinds of multiplexers. The first kind, **Frequency Division Multiplexing** (FDM) is hardly ever used anymore, so we'll only mention it briefly. The third kind, known as **Statistical Multiplexing** (Stat Muxing), is actually only an advanced version of the second kind, called **Time Division Multiplexing** (TDM). So really, you only need to worry about one kind of multiplexing. Easier than you thought.

FDM

FDM is the oldest form of multiplexing. It's the only analog multiplexing technique, so modems aren't required. The voice-grade bandwidth is subdivided by the multiplexer into multiple low-speed channels that are separated to prevent crosstalk between channels. In this way, each channel carries a low-speed line (low-speed because the narrower the bandwidth, the slower the transmission rate). The top speed of an FDM high speed link is only 100 bps. And, as with multiplexed modems, the sum of the terminal transmission speeds cannot exceed the speed of the high-speed link (figure 7-3).

Because the bandwidth can be divided into just so many data channels, FDM can only support a small number of devices. As you may have guessed already, FDM is most effective with low-speed, asynchronous terminals.

One of the benefits of FDM, and of all multiplexing for that matter, is that it allows dumb asynchronous terminals to be clustered, or grouped together, in order to share the same phone line. This is not a multipoint environment, though, because the terminals still are not addressable and so cannot be polled. Because of its many limitations, FDM is considered an inflexible, outmoded multiplexing technique for voice-grade lines.

FDM divides the voicegrade bandwidth of the phone line into low-speed channels. Each terminal is assigned a particular channel. Notice that with FDM, modems are not required because these are analog devices.

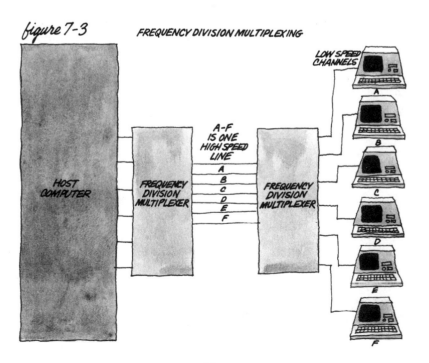

figure 7-3   FREQUENCY DIVISION MULTIPLEXING

TDM

The multiplexing technique used with multi-channel muxed modems is time division multiplexing or TDM. Unlike FDM, it operates digitally, so modems are required on the point-to-point line. (Note: time division multiplexers also exist as stand-alone devices.)

A TDM interleaves bits from synchronous terminals or characters from asynchronous terminals to transmit continually down the leased line at a speed equal to or less than the sum of the separate terminal transmission speeds. Using bit-interleaving, the high-speed link can transmit data at the modems' top speed (e. g., 9600, 14,400 bps, etc.) because the entire bandwidth is used rather than subchannels.

Each terminal is assigned a particular time slot on the high-speed line whether it has something to

TDM interleaves bits or characters to transmit continually down the high-speed line at a speed equal to or less than the sum of the separate terminal transmission speeds.

transmit or not. The order in which the terminals transmit never changes. The TDM operates by scanning the terminals, sampling the first bit or character from each terminal transmission as it goes. It then repeats the process, starting with the first terminal again, sampling the second bit or character and so on.

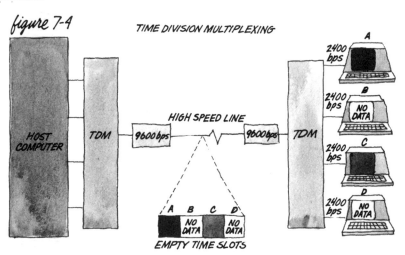

figure 7-4   TIME DIVISION MULTIPLEXING

HIGH SPEED LINE

HOST COMPUTER — TDM — 9600 bps — 9600 bps — TDM

2400 bps — A
2400 bps — B — NO DATA
2400 bps — C
2400 bps — D — NO DATA

A B C D
NO DATA   NO DATA

EMPTY TIME SLOTS

The procedure continues until the multiplexer has sampled all of the different messages from each of the terminals. The demuxing TDM samples each bit or character in order and distributes each terminal's data to its corresponding computer port (figure 7-4).

This may sound like polling but it's not. We're no longer operating in a multipoint network; rather it's point-to-point. And the terminals are transmitting on their own, without an invitation from the host. The TDM is simply allocating time on the high-speed line for each terminal regardless of whether it has data to transmit.

Think of it as a revolving door. The people using the door to get from point A to point B are the "data" filling the "slots" in the door. But the door keeps moving even if some of the slots are empty.

TDM, though, is more flexible than FDM, allowing you to manually change the number or speed of the time slots to some extent as network requirements change. It can also buffer a complete character before transmitting it so that start/stop bits can be removed before asynchronous data is transmitted. This leaves more room on the line for actual information. Despite the added feature of buffers, a TDM cannot retransmit-on-error because transmission is continuous.

In general, FDM is used for lower speed asynchronous, full-duplex, leased line transmission. TDM on the other hand is used for synchronous or asynchronous, full-duplex, leased line transmission.

STATISTICAL MULTIPLEXING
Statistical or intelligent multiplexing is simply an advanced form of TDM. What makes it so interesting is the fact that it does the "impossible." Imagine pouring the entire contents of a gallon container into a quart bottle without spilling a drop. This illustration may seem like a slight exaggeration but it describes exactly what stat muxing does. Remember we said that the sum of the transmission speeds couldn't be more than the speed of the single voice-grade line? Well, with stat muxing, it can.

TDM is inefficient for high-speed transmission because it's continually allocating time for terminals that have nothing to transmit. Terminals very rarely need to transmit continuously at maximum speed. As a matter of fact, many buffered terminals only need to transmit two percent of the time they're in use. And terminals connected to a multiplexer operate simultaneously perhaps only 20 percent of the time.

Statistical multiplexers dynamically allocate time slots only as the terminals require them so that the sum of the individual terminal transmission rates can exceed the speed of the high-speed link.

Stat muxes take advantage of this idle time by "dynamically" allocating time slots only as the terminals require them—on a demand basis. This way, more terminals can be served without increasing the speed of the high-speed line (figure 7-5).

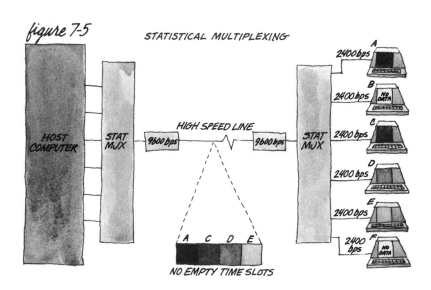

figure 7-5

STATISTICAL MULTIPLEXING

HOST COMPUTER — STAT MUX — 9600 bps — HIGH SPEED LINE — 9600 bps — STAT MUX

A 2400 bps
B 2400 bps — NO DATA
C 2400 bps
D 2400 bps
E 2400 bps
F 2400 bps — NO DATA

A C D E

NO EMPTY TIME SLOTS

So what stat muxing is really doing is betting that too many terminals won't want to transmit simultaneously—like overselling tickets with the anticipation that not everyone will show up. Except it works because stat muxes also have buffers which will temporarily hold the spill-over of data, even during peak periods of traffic. And if the buffers fill, then the stat mux temporarily inhibits some of the terminals from transmitting. Again, to your users, the stat muxes in the network are entirely transparent. Your terminals operate as if connected directly with the host.

Stat muxes typically use an HDLC-type protocol which utilizes a GO BACK N ARQ scheme. This scheme provides an automatic request to repeat the message in the event transmission errors are detected by the receiving stat mux. In this way, error-free communication is maintained, even in the presence of transmission problems.

DATA COMPRESSION

To fit even more information on the line and further increase throughput, stat muxes can actually compress the data being transmitted.

Here's an example of how data compression works. The letter "A" is used much more frequently than the letter "Z". So the 8-bit code for "A" is replaced by a 4-bit representation, and the 8-bit code for "Z" with a 12-bit representation. Again, stat muxing is betting you'll use more "A"s than "Z"s in your transmissions.

In terms of actual performance, stat muxes can transmit four times as much asynchronous data and nearly twice as much synchronous data as other muxing techniques. Using data compression further increases throughput by another 20 to 30 percent. So taking an asynchronous situation as an example, four 9600 bps terminals could transmit over one 9600 bps high-speed line, though the sum of the individual terminal speeds adds up to 38,400 bps (figure 7-6).

Stat muxes interact with various protocols from a mix of terminals to determine which devices have data to send. In other words, they are protocol-sensitive. TDMs, however, are designed only to allocate time slots and not check the terminals for data; so they are not protocol sensitive. What's more, a TDM is easy to implement and usually costs less than a statistical multiplexer because it is not required to have data processing capabilities. In short, time-division muxing is a simple, rock-solid technology that's been working in networks of all types and sizes for many years.

Statistical multiplexers use data compression to further increase throughput up to an additional 30%. In this particular situation, the sum of the transmission rates of these four terminals is four times the speed of the high-speed line.

Delay sensitive applications (e.g., many SDLC applications) are also handled better by TDM because there's always an available slot on the high-speed line. With stat muxing, however, your terminals contend for that slot. If no space is available, your data waits in the buffer, creating delay. Stat muxing can introduce substantial delay in both directions, which would make it a poor choice for certain multipoint, polled applications as well.

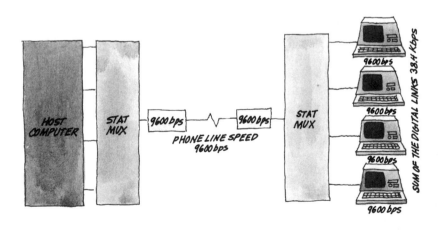

Remember we said Chapter 1 was the road map? Welcome to the crossroads. Up to this point, technology has been basically point-to-point and very cooperative for those of you new to data communications. Well, hang on to your pocket protectors because it gets real exciting from this point on.

Don't worry, the last seven chapters have given you all the foundation you need for a full appreciation. Just wait until you're in a room of people; the conversation suddenly lags, and you start talking about something like, say—digital services. Guaranteed you'll enjoy instant celebrity status. No need to thank us. On to potential fame.

8

CHOOSING THE DIGITAL SERVICE TO MEET YOUR NEEDS

OR

finding the perfect 01

It was just a matter of economics and time. Economics, to provide the cost justification. Time, to develop sophisticated digital transmission products to provide the kind of speed, flexibility, quality, and transmission reliability for your data, voice, video, teleconferencing, and facsimile communications you always dreamed about (don't worry, not everyone can remember their dreams).

More than 20 years ago, the telephone company developed digital transmission facilities to meet its own needs. It began installing digital lines between central offices to replace or augment analog lines already in place. Two principal advantages of digital communications made this move inevitable.

First, digital lines offer more dependable operation. To begin with, digital lines are less sensitive to noise and interference. Wire makes a great antenna. Any signal sent over it will pick up whatever electrical interference surrounds the wire. This interference becomes noise, and in analog transmission, is amplified along with the signal. In digital transmission, the signal is amplified but the noise is "discriminated" out and the original signal regenerated.

Analog facilities, as discussed earlier, are also characterized by measurements of phase, frequency, etc. These parameters all fluctuate in response to changes in the environment, e.g., physical condition of the line and the age of the transmission equipment. Digital facilities are mostly resistant to these effects. In short, digital lines usually work very well, or not at all.

The second big advantage of digital communications is that digital transmission equipment uses less expensive electronics. Less circuitry is needed to classify a voltage level as a zero or a one than to analyze an analog signal for amplitudes and frequencies. Because the transmission equipment is less expensive, the telephone company can install more of it for the same cost, increasing capacity while decreasing its own network costs.

Partly driving digital growth and partly driven by it are two more factors. First, **fiber optics** is becoming the transmission medium of choice. The U. S. is fast becoming laced together by fiber cables. Benefits include freedom from electromagnetic interference, higher transmission capacity, and increased security. It would never happen for practical reasons but the capacity of fiber is so enormous that a single pair could carry all the voice traffic between Boston and New York (this includes teenagers calling 900 numbers). Every long distance carrier is installing new fiber optic facilities, and digital transmitters and receivers have become the standard.

The second point is that ISDN (Integrated Services Digital Network) is by definition digital. We'll talk about this more in a moment (unless you manage to put this book down) but the ISDN standard, which defines a national and international network for voice, video, data, fax, and anything else that can be sent over a line, is digital from the ground up.

Now, AT&T and other carriers are converting many of their analog facilities to digital. Should you run right out and scrap your modems? No. The San Andreas Fault may drop a chunk of California into the ocean some day but you'll notice no one's moving right away. The changeover to digital is subtle. Besides, analog equipment will always provide important applications. Though telephone central offices have "switched to digital" (a little CO joke), they're still perfectly compatible with the analog networks connected to them.

Generally, although there is digital service starting at 2400 bps, digital picks up where high-speed analog leaves off. Therefore, the benefits of digital service are best realized if you're continuously transmitting large volumes of data. Our point is that digital transmission is not necessarily "better" than analog. Think about your application. You're looking for a cost-effective match between your requirements and available technology. Going back to the car analogy, why pay for racing tires if you never drive fast?

Let's start with low-speed, low-volume digital transmission and work our way up. To begin with, as in all communications, "data pumps" are required. In the digital world, **Data Service** and **Channel Service Units** (DSU/CSUs) are the counterpart of analog modems. They're actually baseband "modems" required for any data transmission over all-digital links. More often than not, you'll find a DSU and a CSU combined in a single unit built into larger digital transmission products. This eliminates the need for stand-alone units at each end of your transmission path. Today, for greater network design flexibility, analog modems are being designed so they can become DSU/CSUs with just a software upgrade.

DDS SERVICE

Dataphone Digital Service (DDS), the most basic digital offering, is a full digital link available from AT&T Communications connecting one user facility to another.

In terms of benefits, DDS gets rid of the noise problems associated with analog transmission that we discussed earlier. And because there's usually no analog to digital conversion required for data to reach its destination, digital transmission has a lower bit-error rate than straight analog link transmission. In fact digital transmission offers an accuracy rate of 99.5%. But DDS also has its own unique limitations. For one thing, DDS and other digital services like it are not yet available in all parts of the country. Also, unlike analog transmission, users can only subscribe to DDS at one fixed speed at a time: 2400 bps, 4800 bps, 9600 bps, 19.2 Kbps or 56 Kbps.

DDS comes in two flavors, DDS-I and DDS-II. Rather than degrade slowly, as analog lines often do before they totally fail, DDS-I digital lines usually go out all at once. In other words, it's binary, on or off—great data transmission or no data transmission. What's more, there's typically no inherent dial backup to re-establish the digital connection, and repair can be a long and difficult process. An option to ensure uninterrupted communications using DDS 1 service is to install a separate dial modem network to provide digital-to-analog backup from end-to-end.

DDS-II is a relatively new offering from AT&T, the Bell Operating Companies (BOCs) and other telco carriers. It differs from DDS-I in that it offers the same services plus a **side channel** or **secondary channel**. A what? Briefly, here's how it works. In the analog world, as we discussed, bandwidth is finite; there's just so much usable bandwidth to pump the data through. Using various transmission schemes, it's possible to carve out a small secondary channel from the primary data channel to carry diagnostic information, without interrupting the flow of primary data. (Most network control and management systems use this secondary channel to monitor the data network *nonintrusively*.) The alternative is interrupting main channel data to run diagnostics on the network, which is unacceptable. It would be like continually halting rush hour traffic: the cars will bottleneck.

SWITCHED 56 SERVICE

For voice and data applications that require high transmission rates but don't demand a full-time connection, **Switched 56** is a good flexible solution. It's a digital 56 Kbps service available from AT&T over ACCUNET® Switched 56 lines. Conceptually, it's almost like "digital dial line" service—high-speed transmission on demand.

Switched 56 service is available from AT&T (ACCUNET® Switched 56 and Software Defined Network), US Sprint (VPN 56) and others.

figure 8-1

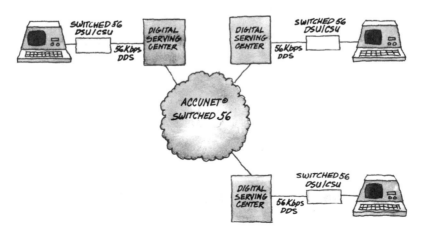

81

Remember, we said a drawback of digital service is that there's no inherent dial backup capability as in analog applications. Well, Switched 56 service provides digital backup capabilities. The Switched 56 devices (essentially a DSU/CSU with a dial pad) connect to the AT&T ACCUNET Switched 56 services for temporary high bandwidth support as needed (figure 8-1). Should the leased DDS line fail, a temporary connection through the Switched 56 network restores full bandwidth service until the private line is repaired.

Fifty-six Kbps used to be very fast. It still is, but now, for applications requiring more bandwidth there's faster—and even *faster.* In recent years, we've seen the emergence of bulk digital capacity offerings from communications carriers. Let's take a look at some examples.

T1/E1 SERVICE

Digital services have evolved based on increments of the *Digital Signal.* DS0 is 64 Kbps, DS1 is 1.544 Mbps (or **T1**), DS2 is 6.312 Mbps (or **T2,** though generally not available), DS3 is 44.736 Mbps (or **T3**), etc.

With T1, digital signals are combined or multiplexed so that two pairs of wire can carry 24 voice or data conversations. These are the same two pairs of wires that can only carry one voice conversation using analog technology. With each conversation running at 64 Kbps, plus 8 Kbps for network control overhead, the total (aggregate) output of T1 is 1.544 Mbps (million bits per second). Conceptually, that's a big "pipe."

Is T1 available around the world? To some extent. It's used in North America and Japan, but in Europe, the CCITT calls it **E1**. E1 specifications differ from T1 in that the aggregate trunk speed is 2.048 Mbps, which is 32 channels at 64 Kbps. Of the 32 channels, 30 are used for voice, one for framing (to be discussed shortly), and one for signalling information.

How does T1/E1 work? To be very basic indeed, information is encoded using time division multiplexing (TDM) for data and **Pulse Code Modulation** (PCM) for voice. PCM digitizes voice when it's carried over digital circuits between the carriers' switches.

Originally, T1 was used by carriers and telcos to link central offices. Today, customers are increasingly using T1 facilities to reduce their telecommunications costs, consolidate their separate voice and data networks, increase their network capacity, and enhance network control and manageability. While data distribution beyond a hub site is best handled by modems and smaller multiplexers, T1 multiplexers and lines offer efficient, economical inter-hub circuits known in the industry as **trunks** or **backbones** to carry larger volumes of data (figure 8-2).

Recent developments in the last few years have made high-capacity T1 lines even more attractive. First, as a result of divestiture and the resulting competition, carriers now price their services in relation to the cost of providing them (a startling new concept). And, as we said, telephone companies can provide T1 service less expensively than they can provide conventional analog service with comparable capacity. Second, because of the first reason, telecommunications equipment manufacturers are now offering multiplexers that allow customers to take advantage of these less expensive T1 lines.

Designing networks using T1 links between hubs offers several advantages. T1 links give you much greater control to configure the network immediately, provided there's additional bandwidth available. Applications can be quickly added and dropped. That means you can schedule the use of T1 lines according to time-dependent demands. So rather than wait for a new phone line to, say, link up with a remote office, all you do is establish the connection using available T1 bandwidth. In the event of line outages, it is the ability of the T1 multiplexer to immediately reroute data that make private T1 networks so attractive. This same principle of re-routing is applied to **load balancing**, where transmissions can be automatically redistributed among resources to avoid transmission congestion and bottlenecks.

figure 8-2

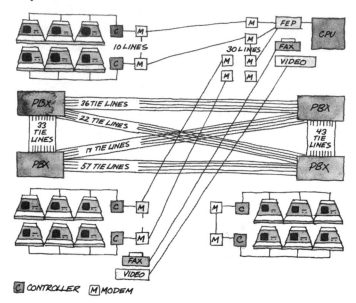

A lot of lines that together can cost a small
fortune. . .

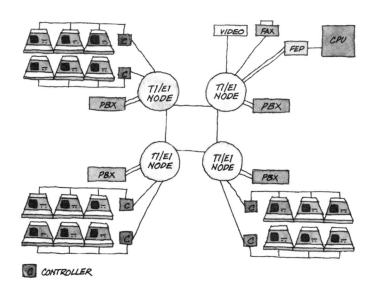

. . . can be consolidated into a single, elegant
T1/E1 backbone capable of supporting the whole
network—resulting in significantly fewer lines and
much lower phone bills.

To summarize, of all the digital services, T1 especially offers the ability to combine applications over the same circuit and route/reroute them as necessary. When properly applied in networking design, T1 can enhance the capacity of your network, reduce networking costs, and bring more of the control of the network within your reach. And easier administration of the telephone companies' lines is one more incentive for installing a T1 network. After all, it's easier to approve a phone bill of ten T1 lines than try to keep track of thousands of lower speed lines.

FRAMING

Not quite so spellbinding as the previous discussion, but important to a full and lasting appreciation of T1, is the topic of **framing**. Framing has little to do with interior decorating and a lot to do with Chapter 3—only on a much larger scale. We're talking about packaging data so it's read correctly. In this case, the DTEs are T1 multiplexers.

Ready for a little math? There's no pop quiz. Between us, just follow the logic. We want you to get to the point where you can appreciate the extended superframe (sounds a little like something you'd buy for a '67 Impala, doesn't it?).

As we said, T1 technology was originally based on multiplexing 24 voice channels on two twisted pairs. Each channel carries digitized voice plus signaling information in 8-bit bytes, so a frame is formatted, consisting of 192 (that's 8 x 24) bits of information. In addition, to identify each frame, a framing bit or "flag" is added in the 193rd bit position. With each byte updated 8,000 times a second, the transmission speed of T1 is (193 x 8,000) or 1.544 Mbps. Whew! Now for the easy part.

Any information going out into the T1 world must adhere to the framing format just described, which is known as **D4 frame and format**. (The "frame" is the sequence of 193 bits, the "format" means that the 192 information bits are divided into 24 8-bit channels.) Now let's shift gears and think in terms of time rather than space. Instead of 24 "channels" think of them as 24 "time slots" with your data hurtling through at 1.544 Mbps. Remember, that includes 8,000 framing bits per second, or one framing bit every 125 microseconds. To recognize all those framing bits in a high-speed bit stream, the receiving T1 mux looks for a predetermined sequence of ones and zeros that repeats every 12 frames. These twelve frames make up a **superframe** (figure 8-3). In other words, every 2,316 bits (12 x 193) a new superframe begins. In addition, within each superframe, other bits are "robbed" for additional signaling information, such as dialing information and line supervision. This process, known as **robbed bit signaling**, sacrifices insignificant bits of user information to accommodate the signaling information necessary to complete the transmission successfully.

The extended superframe (ESF) doubles the number of signaling bits available and is gradually supplanting the D4 or superframe format.

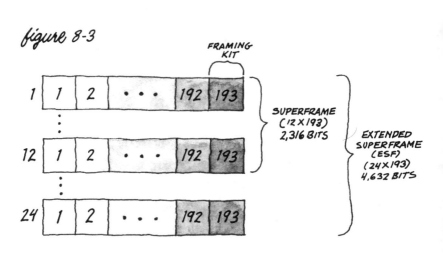

figure 8-3

The problem is that D4 framing and robbed bit signaling were really developed for voice communication, where changing a bit here and a bit there wouldn't really matter much. Now, however, with T1 being increasingly used for data, it's difficult to find bits to rob. Bit error rates can have a disastrous impact on reliable data transmission. Hence the need for the **extended superframe** or **ESF**. ESF increases the size of the superframe from 12 to 24 frames, doubling the number of signaling bits available (figure 8-3). Moreover, instead of needing 8,000 framing bits, ESF uses only 2,000. That leaves 6,000 bits in that 193rd bit position for other functions such as error checking and network information.

As early as 1979, AT&T proposed that the ESF be implemented on its T1 circuits in order to provide in-service diagnostic capability. T1 is a tariffed service and the tariff guarantees the customer a specific standard of performance. With D4 framing there is no way to truly measure this performance without taking the line out of service. ESF provides carriers and T1 service users with a means of obtaining a true measurement of system performance without interrupting the flow of information on the line, and this means real-time testing for errors.

So to review, the T1 environment is currently in the midst of a major change in framing format. The D4 or Superframe (SF) format is being supplanted by the Extended Superframe (ESF) format. The key advantage of ESF is the designation of portions of the overhead bandwidth for diagnostics and real-time performance monitoring—with no decreases in information bandwidth.

FRACTIONAL T1 SERVICE

We said we'd cover digital services from smallest to largest but here's a slight digression. In a T1 network, you lease a T1 circuit between two hubs or locations and you transmit on the entire T1 bandwidth of the 24 DS0s (remember, that's 24 x 64 Kbps channels plus 8 Kbps or 1.544 Mbps). Previously, if you didn't want that much bandwidth, you had to make do with a 56 Kbps line which, on the other hand, might not provide enough capacity.

In a **Fractional T1** (FT1) network (similar to European **Nx64** high-speed digital services), you can lease a portion of the 24 DS0s on a T1 link. For example, if an application requires only eight DS0s (that's 8 x 64 Kbps or 512 Kbps), you could lease DS0-0 through DS0-7. Because you contract only for the bandwidth needed for an application, FT1 can provide a substantial cost savings.

In a Fractional T1 network (or Nx64 in Europe), you can lease a portion of the 24 DS0s on a T1 link. Here, the multiplexed channels originating at the host site are switched to two different destinations using a DACS network.

As with T1, FT1 networks also allow the switching of DS0s within the network, giving you greater flexibility and economy when configuring multipoint networks. Multiplexed communication channels originating at one customer location may be switched to two different destinations within the network using a DACS (Digital Access Cross-connect Switch) network (figure 8-4).

figure 8-4

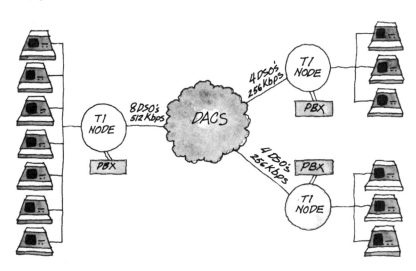

T1 FAST PACKET TECHNOLOGY

Since 1982, when AT&T first offered T1 to the public as a tariffed service (later called ACCUNET T1.5), T1 lines have become more available and much more affordable. That being the case, it makes sense to streamline your company's voice, data, facsimile, and video traffic into a single T1 backbone. Besides the obvious savings in line costs, consolidation simplifies network management. A single digital T1 backbone is easier to control, troubleshoot, and maintain than separate analog networks.

How well your T1s support your network has to do with how your information is routed onto the T1 backbone and that's where **fast packet technology** has made a critical contribution.

Fast packet nodes (in this case, the nodes are actually T1 multiplexers) acting as nodal processors, deliver tremendous cost savings while addressing the critical networking requirements of your business. Bottom line, T1 can save you money. But combined with fast packet technology, you save more money and improve networking efficiency by using fewer T1 lines to reliably consolidate your transmissions.

The two major benefits of fast packet technology are *efficiency* and *resiliency*. A T1 line transmitting at 1.544 Mbps gives you a lot of bandwidth and fast packet technology provides an extremely efficient way to make use of it. In fact, fast packet can be many times more cost-effective for today's voice and data intensive networks than traditional time division multiplexers (also known as circuit switches), which is the conventional type of nodal processor used in T1 networks.

A circuit-switched TDM divides the T1 bandwidth (1.544 Mbps) into 24 fixed time slots or channels of 64 Kbps, allocating one slot to each of 24 voice or data channels feeding into the node. But in a typical phone conversation, for example, natural pauses in speech account for up to 60 percent of transmission time—so you're paying to transmit silence. Fast packet allocates bandwidth instantaneously on an as-needed basis instead of relying on fixed channel allotments (figure 8-5).

By suppressing the silences in voice conversations and idle characters in data transmissions, fast packet technology provides a significant improvement in bandwidth efficiency. For voice, this equates to a two-to-one improvement or the ability to double the number of 64 Kbps voice channels. In addition, some vendors offer ADPCM, which gives you an additional two-to-one compression as well as another 24 channels. Instead of a two-to-one compression, now you can have four-to-one compression. And that means 24 x 4, or 96 voice calls running over a single T1 line (or 120 on an E1 link) —a 400 percent increase in throughput without compromising quality. Fast packet technology is also ideal for "bursty" data applications like LANs, high-resolution graphic workstations, and host-to-

In a circuit-switched T1/E1 network, bandwidth is divided into fixed channel allotments. Fast packet technology, on the other hand, allocates bandwidth on an as-needed basis, which translates into fewer T1/E1 circuits needed to support your applications—and fewer monthly carrier bills.

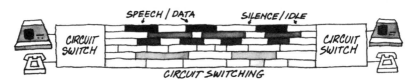

host connections. Again, by suppressing idles, between two-to-one and three-to-one efficiency can be achieved.

We mentioned resiliency earlier. Fast packet is good under normal conditions but it's great in a crisis because it's *virtually* impossible to prevent the information from getting through. Here's why.

With fast packet, you don't have to worry about a T1 link failure affecting network availability. Fast packet is resilient or "self-healing" when used in ring or mesh topologies (we'll get to those in Chapter 10), so in the event of a failure information can be easily rerouted across the network in seconds without noticeable delay. This ability to immediately reroute traffic is due in large part to fast packet's unique frame format, again, the way in which bits of voice or data are organized for transmission across the T1 line (figure 8-6).

Like TDM, fast packet technology sends information along T1 circuits using D4 framing. There are, however, different ways to organize those 193 bits within the frame. Traditional T1 technology formats them into 24 discrete time slots or DS0s, allocating one DS0 to each device connected to the node. Fast packet does something quite different. Each fast packet traveling across the backbone carries information destined for a single channel only.

Fast packet technology dedicates the entire frame or packet to only one user and puts a destination address at the end. With one user per frame and each frame addressed, whole packets can be sent to their destinations via virtual circuits. And the entire frame does not have to be disassembled and reassembled to pass through an intermediate node. With traditional circuit switching, a single frame carries information from 24 circuits. And instead of assigning a virtual circuit to an entire frame (like fast packet does), the circuit switched node instead assigns a fixed route to each DS0 within the frame.

With traditional D4 frame and format circuit switching, routing table algorithms can introduce a slight delay that's normally transparent to the user. But when a T1 link or circuit switched backbone goes down, this little delay can stretch because the remaining nodes suddenly have to update their routing table algorithms as well. In large circuit switched networks, this procedure will take many minutes during which calls will be terminated and transactions lost.

In a fast packet network, an alternate route is a detour that redirects entire packets around a problem and along a continuous path, using whatever bandwidth is available.

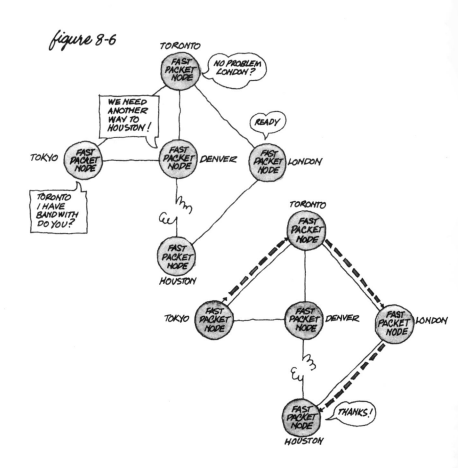

figure 8-6

But with fast packet technology, because bandwidth is allocated dynamically, entire packets of control information can be transmitted as they're needed, taking only as much T1 bandwidth as required. By speeding the delivery of control information at this magnitude, alternate paths are set up that much sooner, and fast packets are simply redirected around the problem along a continuous path—taking advantage of available bandwidth.

For a more detailed discussion, read Motorola Codex's *Applications Booklet of T1 Fast Packet Technology.*

FRAME RELAY

Do all new technologies begin with the letter" F?" No, but here's another. **Frame relay** is related to fast packet switching in that it provides an ideal network access technology for bringing data onto a fast packet switching backbone.

Frame relay is a data-only network access standard—switching within the network is not specified by the frame relay standard. Frame relay has evolved out of the growing need for a data protocol designed to handle emerging high-speed applications, such as large file transfers, imaging, and graphics transmission. These applications transmit data in variable burst sizes and unpredictable timing patterns; consequently, they cannot be efficiently handled by traditional protocols. Frame relay, on the other hand, is specifically designed to efficiently manage such data traffic.

Frame relay is based on the X.25 protocol (covered in the next chapter: in fact, you might want to come back to frame relay after getting acquainted with X.25). They are similar in that both are packet mode network access protocols that utilize addressed frames of information of various lengths, which can be multiplexed from different sources over a single physical interface.

Frame relay, however, is different from X.25 in that it takes advantage of high-speed digital networks in order to provide greater throughput, lower-delay switching that is ideally suited for applications such as connecting high-speed local area networks over the wide area network (see Chapter 10 for more on LANs). Because digital transmission services have better error performance and end systems are increasingly more intelligent, frame relay is not burdened with error recovery overhead and relies on the end systems for that function. Without the overhead associated with error processing, frame relay increases throughput capacity and can support higher speeds (compared to traditional X.25).

In fact, frame relay supports speeds up to 2 Mbps. In some cases, frame relay is an alternative to X.25, but it also complements X.25 in a number of applications. With the standards nearing completion, frame relay is receiving exceptional attention from network suppliers, carriers, and users, and is likely to be the method of choice for high-speed network access throughout the 1990s.

For a more detailed discussion, see Motorola Codex's *Basics Book of Frame Relay.*

ISDN
Ever wonder about a future where you can tap as easily into a worldwide data network as plugging an appliance into an electrical outlet (without using those three-prong adapters)?

Well the future is here, or at least well on its way. **ISDN** stands for Integrated Services Digital Network (and it doesn't even begin with the letter "F."). The aim of ISDN is to implement a universal datacomm network that provides end-to-end connectivity over digital lines. A network where all of today's separate transmission services are integrated and accessed via a common set of interface standards through a single plug in your wall. A network that can move data, voice, image, and facsimile either separately or simultaneously over the same pair of copper wires already in place today.

What's driving the development of ISDN? For years, users have been demanding a solution to problems with incompatible equipment, protocols, and interfaces; frustrations over delays; the need to cut costs by making better use of leased lines; the need to back up leased lines without the costs of maintaining redundant links; and the need for increased transmission capacity. The wish list goes on and on. And like the traveling salesman in the cowboy movies who brings his wagon into town, selling elixirs that cure everything from backache to bunions, ISDN has come to town, so to speak. Only ISDN is real. Well, mostly. You see, in many cases ISDN is still in development, but implementation has already started, and it's looking like a better bet every day.

As a switched service, ISDN is just as attractive to the telephone companies. It is basic to the operation of any carrier that it use switched circuits more than leased lines. Switched circuits are more profitable because the same facility can be sold to many customers rather than to just one. And of course, public networks are designed for switched circuits. For some time, telecommunications authorities worldwide have been paving the way for ISDN implementation. Now it's just a matter of waiting for the carriers to offer cost-effective ISDN services. Vendors are already including ISDN capabilities in their products in anticipation.

Two large forces are at work here. *Competition* has brought us a wealth of incompatible DTE and DCE equipment with proprietary protocols. And *Evolution* is happening throughout our communications links. For one thing, as we keep saying, the world is slowly going digital. And as we discussed, digital networks are cheaper to build and maintain.

Another reason for the shift to ISDN is that currently in the workplace, 90% of phone line usage is for voice and only 10% for data. By the mid 1990s, this should even out to 50/50, drawing on the greater capacity that only digital can provide. With these new demands, many feel ISDN is the solution for putting more data through the system, more reliably, with more flexibility, at a lower cost.

As defined by the CCITT, services fall into three categories: **Bearer services** (getting information from here to there), **Teleservices** (information processing services provided to the user for a fee), and **Supplementary services** (those that enhance either of the previous two). Standard ISDN services include voice communication, circuit and packet switched data communications (we'll discuss packet switching in the next chapter), switched and nonswitched circuits, text message services, and facsimile. Future services to look forward to are enhanced voice communications, home telemetry, and videotex services (figure 8-7).

The CCITT, to maximize flexibility and competition for all communications functions, has identified the points across the communications link where functions come together. The goal is to establish a universal standard at each of those interfaces. In practical terms, this means that products performing the same functions will ultimately be compatible, regardless of vendor.

In an ISDN network, voice, data, video, facsimile, etc., share one digital link, which provides access to a wide range of services.

Access to the ISDN network will be through these standard multipurpose interfaces.

Up until recently, datacomm vendors attempted to establish proprietary standards that their competitors couldn't copy. Users were

figure 8-7

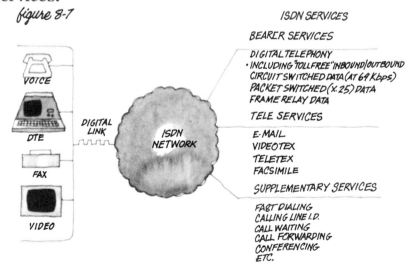

ISDN SERVICES

BEARER SERVICES

DIGITAL TELEPHONY
• INCLUDING "TOLLFREE" INBOUND/OUTBOUND
CIRCUIT SWITCHED DATA (AT 64 Kbps)
PACKET SWITCHED (X.25) DATA
FRAME RELAY DATA

TELE SERVICES

E-MAIL
VIDEOTEX
TELETEX
FACSIMILE

SUPPLEMENTARY SERVICES

FAST DIALING
CALLING LINE I.D.
CALL WAITING
CALL FORWARDING
CONFERENCING
ETC.

VOICE

DTE

FAX

VIDEO

DIGITAL
LINK

ISDN
NETWORK

locked into a single vendor's products. Changing vendors could mean having to scrap the existing network entirely. With ISDN, which incorporates universal open standards, users can choose the "best" product for their application, and through open interfaces vendors can sell into networks traditionally closed to them.

The CCITT has established two ISDN transmission rates. **Basic Rate Interface** (BRI) is where the phone company divides its existing twisted pair local loop into three separate channels: two 64-Kbps "B" channels and one 16-Kbps "D" channel. The B channel carries voice or data and the D channel carries signaling information and low-speed packet data. **Primary Rate Interface** (PRI) for the U.S., Canada and Japan consists of 23 64-Kbps B channels and one 64-Kbps D channel. In Europe, there are 30 B channels and one D channel. With PRI, users can move their data at T1 speed (figure 8-8).

It is the operation of the D channel that distinguishes ISDN from other digital alternatives to the analog network. Signaling in the D channel tells the network how to handle the B channel data. It also

Basic Rate Interface or BRI consists of two 64-Kbps "B" channels and one 16-Kbps "D" channel (2B+D). PRI (23B+D) provides for 23 B channels (U.S., Canada, and Japan) or 30 B channels (Europe) and one 64-Kbps D channel.

figure 8-8

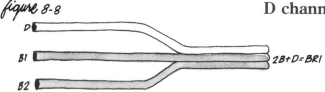

D CHANNEL: SIGNALING + PACKET DATA; B CHANNEL: CLEAR 64 Kbps DIGITAL ACCESS

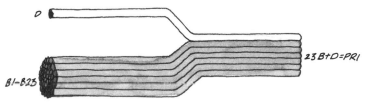

D CHANNEL: SIGNALING; B CHANNEL: CLEAR 64 Kbps DIGITAL ACCESS

ISDN INTERFACES

makes possible supplementary services we discussed and provides the user with call control information. This signaling is what opens and closes switches and routes calls.

Currently, long distance carriers accomplish their signaling *out-of-band* over a separate dedicated network in order to open and close switches, and route calls. It allows them to set up calls more quickly leading to better use of existing channels. The local loop provided by your local carrier uses *in-band* signaling which presents certain difficulties. Tone-based signals compete with voice and data for air time—a real problem when transmitting data and an in-line "beep" destroys the transmission. ISDN solves these difficulties by offering out-of-band signaling on the local loop, plus those many services to choose from, and all from a single pair of wires.

For the time being, let's say ISDN is not the answer to every data communications problem, but it does hold great promise. For a more detailed discussion, read the Motorola Codex *Basics Book of ISDN*.

Whether analog or digital, for the most part, your data has been running down the phone lines, point-to-point, like beads through a straw. If the lines are leased, you pay a flat monthly fee based on bandwidth and distance. If you're using dial lines, you pay based on time as well as distance.

What if you didn't have to pay on time or distance? What if all you had to worry about was the three feet of wire hanging off the back of your terminal and the network worried about the rest? What if sending data were as simple as mailing a letter—just address it and the mail system takes care of the rest (well, usually)? Then you'd be talking X.25. Seriously, did you ever think you'd be talking X.25?

9

WITH
X.25 YOU
CAN TRANSMIT
VIRTUALLY
ANYWHERE
OR

your PAD or mine

No, X.25 is not something new from NASA. Instead, it refers to a data communications standard (you'd think it would at least have a nicer name). Anyway, up until now, we've been discussing point-to-point technologies. X.25 is pointless. Let's rephrase that: Unlike point-to-point technology, with X.25 you can transmit *virtually* anywhere.

TECHNOLOGY VS. STANDARDS

Packet switching is a networking technology in which
the data from many different users is divided into small
units called packets and transmitted over a common
transmission line. The growth of distributed networks
and the drive towards universal data communications
standards have made packet switching an increasingly
attractive network solution. The benefits are greater
connectivity, sharing of host resources and transmission facilities, standardized network access, indepen-
dence from single vendor proprietary solutions, interfaces to public data networks, expandability, and
comprehensive network control and management.
Sounds like it addresses just about everything,
doesn't it?

Then what's X.25? **X.25** is an internationally
accepted protocol—a way to format information with an
address and handling instructions, much like a letter
being sent via the post office. The X.25 protocol allows
terminals and computers to be connected to a packet
switched data network (PSDN). Today, users with
widely dispersed populations of terminals requiring a
high degree of connectivity are turning to X.25 solutions. To keep things simple, in this chapter we'll be
using the terms "X.25" and "packet switching"
interchangeably.

VIRTUAL CONNECTION

We've used the word *virtually* before. Packet switching
differs from **circuit switching** (regular dedicated
phone lines discussed throughout the book) because it
uses **virtual circuits**. In other words, the connection
made is a *logical* connection, since the virtual circuit is
really bandwidth allocated on demand—not a permanent link between the two parties exchanging data. It's
not quite magic. "Logic" or routing and destination
information (think of it as an address) accompanies
each packet through the network. Basically, since
packet network resources are shared among network
users, packet switching is less expensive than circuit
switching for many applications and provides more efficient use of bandwidth. We'll explain more later.

Packet networks are described as real-time, interactive networks. Since they offer efficient use of circuits, packet networks are best suited to applications where users are geographically dispersed and require connectivity to multiple locations. Packet networks provide the flexibility required for real-time applications; they also provide error correction and can accommodate unscheduled high-volume traffic requirements.

The three kinds of packet networks are *public, private,* and a combination of the two called *hybrid.* All three reduce transmission costs by allowing multiple applications to share the same phone line, by reducing the number of access points, and by allowing you to pay by the packet regardless of distance (rather than the flat circuit switched line rate). Your choice of network depends on application and bandwidth requirements. Large organizations such as transportation, financial services, and government, prefer private or hybrid networking because it provides standards support, greater network security, integration into the public networks, as well as easy migration to future offerings like ISDN.

PACKET NETWORK COMPONENTS

If we took apart a packet network, what would we find? A mess of ones and zeros. Perhaps, but actually there are five components to a packet network for you to be concerned about: **LAC** (local access components), **PAD** (packet assemblers/disassemblers), **PN** (packet switching nodes), **NL** (network links), and **NMS** (network management system). See figure 9-1.

Local access components such as a terminal, line, and modem move the data intended for transmission to the nearby PAD. The PAD provides access to the network and ensures compatibility between different user devices and the packet switched network. In all cases, the output must be standardized before going to the PN. The PAD "packetizes" the data from the terminal and sends it on to the PN for routing. In addition to creating packets, PADs also "depacketize" data when it arrives, before sending it on to the receiving terminal. Other functions performed by PADs include physical line concentration, call setup, protocol conversion, code conversion, protocol emulation, and making the network operator's shoulders look bigger (a little fashion joke).

PNs route each packet to its proper destination. The PNs also handle billing, perform network diagnostics, and make gateway connections. To ensure the highest availability, PNs are often installed in redundant configurations.

The NL or physical circuit connects the PNs to each other. This linkage can be handled through different media such as analog or digital circuits, and

A packet switched data network consists of five major groups of network components.

microwave or satellite systems. Speeds range from 9600 bps to T1. A little jargon: NLs are often referred to as the **backbone**

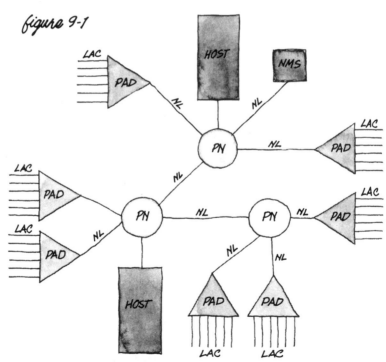

figure 9-1

LEGEND - PN: PACKET SWITCHING NODE PAD: PACKET ASSEMBLER / DISASSEMBLER
NMS: NETWORK MANAGEMENT SYSTEM LAC: LOCAL ACCESS COMPONENT
NL: NETWORK LINK

packet network or **backbone layer** while the PADs are referred to as the **access network** or **network layer**.

The most critical function of the NMS is maintenance of the network database. Here resides the master copy of all software and configurations for each node as well as routing tables and end-user interface profiles. In the event of a problem, database records can be down-line loaded to a malfunctioning node to "refresh" its memory without requiring onsite technical personnel. From the NMS console, the operator can "watch" or monitor the entire network and perform necessary tasks such as logging alarms indicating network problems, initiating diagnostic tests to pinpoint the causes, taking restoral action, and gathering network performance statistics. (More on network management in Chapter 11.)

TRANSMISSIONS THROUGH A PSDN

You're probably asking yourself right now, how do I send data over a packetized network? You place a call much the way you do a regular voice phone call. A virtual call placed through a packet switching network occurs in three phases. In the *call setup phase,* the caller must establish a connection with a PAD in the area. In the *data transfer phase,* the two users (or user and host) are in full-duplex, real-time communication. In the *call clearing phase,* the transaction is concluded. What's key here is that the network remains transparent to the users. There's no obvious indication what technology is driving the communication. Like we said, the data runs out the back of your terminal and the network worries about the rest.

Another way to look at packet switching is to think of the data you want to transmit as a letter. At the sending end, the PAD tears the letter into pieces and inserts each piece into a different envelope. The network serves as an electronic mail carrier. It doesn't care about the envelope's contents, only the address on the outside. At the receiving end, another PAD reassembles the various pieces back into the original letter.

In a circuit switched network, there's only one way to get from here to there and only one mail carrier. In a packet switched network, there are several. As we discussed, routing determines the proper sequence of PNs and NLs necessary to support the virtual circuit when a call is initiated. Again, the nodes depend on the database to decide the best routes for the packetized data. To protect against failure, packet switching nodes may be interconnected in a *mesh* configuration to facilitate *alternate routing* (figure 9-2). In addition, when there's heavy traffic on a primary route, the switching nodes may choose a secondary route to distribute new traffic and eliminate bottlenecks.

To support each virtual connection, a portion of the total network capacity (nodal processing power,

When key network components are deployed in a redundant or "mesh" configuration, alternate routes are selected transparently to the users.

buffer capacity and bandwidth) is pre-allocated at call setup time. The virtual call then becomes an "advance reservation." With more users and heavier traffic volumes, the NMS may allocate additional nodal capacity or bandwidth to avoid data transport delays and momentary blocking of end user access.

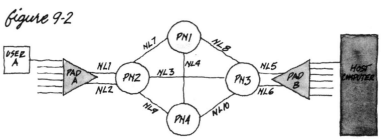

figure 9-2

LEGEND – PN:PACKET SWITCHING NODE   PAD: PACKET ASSEMBLERS/DISASSEMBLERS   NL:NETWORKLINK

X.25 AND THE OSI REFERENCE MODEL

Now that you know *how* a packet switching network works, the question is *why* does it work? The answer is the X.25 protocol. In 1976, the CCITT (remember them?) ratified recommendation X.25, which specifies a set of protocols for connecting terminals and computers to packet switching networks. X.25 (and related Recommendations X.3, X.28, X.29, X.32, X.75, X.96 and X.121) form the basis for present day packet switching. X.25 essentially specifies the format for transmitting data between two devices; for example, between a PAD and a packet network node.

To answer the question on the tip of your tongue, yes, X.25 does conform to the OSI Basic Reference Model. In fact, it will be useful to take the scenic route, so to speak, and arrive at a better understanding of X.25 by way of a detour through OSI.

As we mentioned in Chapter 1, out there in the world there's a group called the ISO, which stands for the International Organization for Standardization. This group consists of representatives of the many constituencies within the wide world of data communications and telecommunications: from vendors to users to carriers.

The OSI Reference Model subdivides overall data communications processes into seven functional layers.

figure 9-3

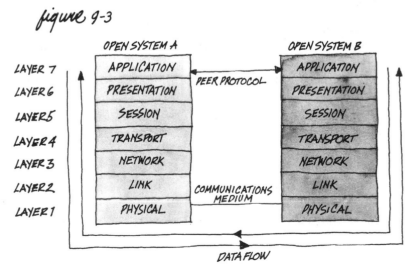

	OPEN SYSTEM A		OPEN SYSTEM B
LAYER 7	APPLICATION	PEER PROTOCOL	APPLICATION
LAYER 6	PRESENTATION		PRESENTATION
LAYER 5	SESSION		SESSION
LAYER 4	TRANSPORT		TRANSPORT
LAYER 3	NETWORK		NETWORK
LAYER 2	LINK	COMMUNICATIONS MEDIUM	LINK
LAYER 1	PHYSICAL		PHYSICAL

DATA FLOW

Among its many activities, the ISO has a committee which is working on a set of communications standards that that will permit communication between equipment from different vendors. This **Open Systems Interconnection** (or **OSI**) committee has developed a **Basic Reference Model** that describes a layer architecture in which overall data communications activities are divided into seven functional "layers" (figure 9-3).

Layers 1 through 3 (the *physical, data link,* and *network* layers) deal with getting data from Point A to Point B over a specific network technology (and to a certain extent, with massaging the information to get it ready for transport). Layers 4 through 7, by contrast, deal with communicating the data independent of the network used. Over the long run, this effort will make it possible for people to exchange data using products from multiple vendors, all of whom have made a commitment to "open" systems and standards, rather than closed (or proprietary) ones. (The interface between each layer standardizes access points so that hardware and software systems can be compatible with each other, regardless of manufacturer.)

Each of the layers of the OSI Basic Reference Model performs a specific data communications task— a service to and for the layer which precedes it (e.g., the network layer provides a service for the transport layer). The process can be likened to placing a letter in a series of envelopes before it's sent through the postal system (a slightly different twist on our earlier postal analogy). Each succeeding envelope adds another layer of processing or overhead information necessary to process the transaction. Together all the envelopes help make sure the letter gets to the right address and that the message received is identical to the message sent. Once the entire package is received at its destination, the envelopes are opened one by one until the letter itself emerges exactly as written (figure 9-4).

In a datacomm transaction, however, each end user is unaware of the envelopes, which perform their functions transparently. For example, we can track an automatic teller machine (ATM) transaction through our multilayer system. One multiple layer system (Open System A) provides an application layer that is an interface to the person attempting a transaction, while the other multiple layer system (Open System B) provides an application layer that interfaces with ATM applications software in the bank's host computer. The corresponding layers in Open Systems A and B are called **peer layers** and communicate through **peer protocols.** These peer protocols provide communication support for the user's application, performing such transaction-related tasks as debiting an account, dispensing currency, or crediting an account.

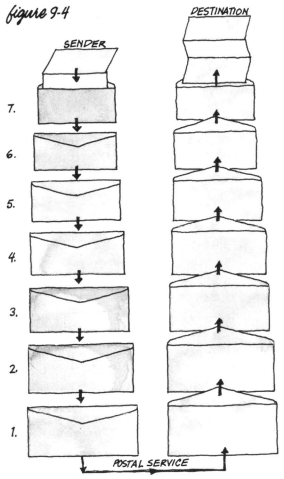

figure 9-4

The OSI Reference Model can be likened to placing a letter in a series of envelopes; each envelope bears information necessary to ensure the letter arrives at its proper address exactly as written. Once the letter reaches its destination, the envelopes are opened one by one, until the letter itself emerges.

Actual data flow between the two real open systems (Open System A and Open System B), however, is from top to bottom in one open system (Open System A, which in this example is the source), across the communications line, and then from bottom to top in the other open system (Open System B, which in this example is the destination). Each time user application data passes downward from one layer to the next in the same sytem, processing information is added. When that information is removed and processed by the peer layer in the other system, it causes various tasks (error correction, flow control, etc.) to be performed. You, the ATM user, are unaware of any of this, of course, but in fact that's what's happening while the words "Please wait, your transaction is being processed" appear on the screen.

To date, the ISO has labored away on all seven of the layers, which are summarized below in the order in which the data actually flows as it leaves the source:

☐ Layer 7, the *application* layer, which provides for a user application (such as getting money from an ATM) to interface with the OSI application layer. This OSI application layer has a corresponding peer layer in the other open system (the bank's host computer);

☐ Layer 6, the *presentation* layer, which makes sure the user information (a request for $50 in cash to be debited from your checking account) is in a format (i.e., syntax or sequence of ones and zeros) the destination open system can understand;

☐ Layer 5, the *session* layer, which provides synchronization control of data between the open systems (i.e., makes sure the bit configurations that pass through layer 5 at the source are the same as those that pass through layer 5 at the destination);

☐ Layer 4, the *transport* layer, which ensures that an end-to-end connection has been established between the two open systems (i.e., layer 4 at

108

the destination "confirms the request for a connection," so to speak, that it has received from layer 4 at the source);

☐ Layer 3, the *network* layer, which provides routing and relaying of data through the network (among other things, at layer 3 on the outbound side an "address" gets slapped on the "envelope" which is then read by layer 3 at the destination);

☐ Layer 2, the *data link* layer, which includes flow control of data as it passes down through this layer in one open system and up through the peer layer in the other open system;

☐ Layer 1, the *physical interface* layer, which includes the ways in which data communications equipment is connected, mechanically and electrically, and the means by which the data moves across those physical connections from layer 1 at the source to layer 1 at the destination.

Admittedly, that was a lengthy detour, but as promised, it brought us back to our discussion of X.25. The three peer protocols described in X.25 correspond to the three bottom layers of the OSI Basic Reference Model (figure 9-5).

Layer One, the physical layer protocol called CCITT X.21, specifies the electrical, mechanical, and procedural requirements to support PSDNs. The North American standard specified by CCITT is called X.21 bis. Now hold onto your PADs, X.21 bis is also known as EIA 232-D. Are you making the connection? In

The three peer protocols of CCITT Recommendation X.25 correspond to the lowest three levels of the OSI Reference Model.

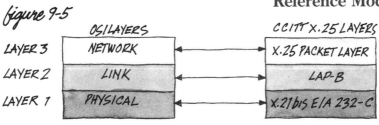

figure 9-5

	OSI LAYERS		CCITT X.25 LAYERS
LAYER 3	NETWORK	◄———►	X.25 PACKET LAYER
LAYER 2	LINK	◄———►	LAP-B
LAYER 1	PHYSICAL	◄———►	X.21 bis EIA 232-C

other words, any device compatible with EIA 232-D is compatible with an X.25 PSDN at Layer One. So at this level, we're talking plug compatible. (When speed requirements exceed 19.2 Kbps on the network side, then CCITT V.35 interface is required.)

Layer Two, the link layer peer protocol called **LAPB** (Link Access Procedure-Balanced—who thinks these names up?) manages the transfer of data frames from one open system to another. The major functions of LAPB are link management using several different frame types; error control to ensure data is transferred across the link accurately; flow control to temporarily stop transmission due to storage or display limitations; and failure recovery. Failure recovery refers to a general OSI principle that higher layers provide a means of recovery for failures in lower layer functions.

Layer Three, the network layer peer protocol, manages the transfer of data packets from one end of an X.25 connection to the other—DTE to DTE. In addition to establishing end-to-end connections, Layer Three establishes addresses and routes, provides flow control, recovers from Layer Two failures, provides optional network service features, and diagnostic functions.

SWITCHING TO X.25

Using your newly acquired expertise in X.25 technology, let's look at packet switching as it applies to real world applications. Three factors we discussed earlier will help you determine the benefit of packet switching for your application: 1. Terminal population dispersion. 2. The need for connectivity. 3. Traffic patterns.

Terminal population dispersion. The more geographically dispersed the terminals are, the more economical packet switching becomes by reducing the number of lines. Packet networks share internodal bandwidth among users, thus reducing the cost per user. In the circuit networks we discussed before, as DTEs move farther apart from each other, transmission costs increase because of distance (just like a phone call). In packet switching, terminals and other DTE devices are connected to nearby PADs and other access devices so you avoid costly distance charges.

The need for connectivity. The more devices you can reach from your terminal, the greater the connectivity of that terminal. And as a rule, the greater the connectivity, the more you save on equipment costs. Leased line networks generally provide little connectivity because you're hardwired into the host either point-to-point or multipoint. For many applications, these leased line configurations are perfectly adequate. X.25 becomes a consideration only when widespread connectivity is required. PSDNs provide virtual access from any networking device to any other networking device using the same protocol in the network.

Traffic patterns. PSDNs fit best in low line usage applications where the data traffic is interactive, transactional, or what's known as "bursty." These are typically human-to-host interactions, characterized by long gaps or idle time between transmissions. An ATM network is a good example. Unlike dedicated bandwidth, which is assigned for some period, idle time or no idle time, PSDNs are cost-effective because they can statistically multiplex data, making maximum use of the bandwidth on a packet by packet basis to fill any gaps with data.

Based on our discussion, here are some examples where packet switching can really pay off: Inquiry/response such as dialing into a database or using electronic mail; electronics funds transfer such as ATMs; wholesale/retail including credit card approval and inventory control; and forms entry like insurance claims and loan applications.

Is packet switching right for your datacomm application? Judge the benefits of X.25 the way you would any other technology: Connectivity, availability, accuracy, flexibility, security, manageability, expandability, and cost-effectiveness. To help you decide, read Motorola Codex's *Basics Book of X.25 Packet Switching.*

So you got your analog lines. You got your digital lines. You got your X.25 network. Now what? Is it just a lot of spaghetti connecting your company to the rest of the world? Say hello to the AN family. There's LAN, MAN and WAN. They have a way of discussing your data amongst themselves that we're sure you'll find interesting. Just keep reading.

10

NETWORK TOPOLOGY

OR

playing connect the dots

Up until this moment, if someone asked you to name the three major networks, you'd probably say ABC, NBC, and CBS. Well, those folks are okay for news, entertainment and violence, but the three major networks that really tie the planet together are LAN, MAN, and WAN.

Local Area Networks, **Metropolitan Area Networks**, and **Wide Area Networks** can also be described conceptually as network topologies—ranging

from short commutes to world travel. They are networking technologies designed to *connect the dots* in
three distinct ways. LANs range from an office floor to
a campus of buildings. MANs link up an entire city. And
WANs span nationally and internationally. Rest assured,
though your data may be continually passing among
these three network topologies, the process is transparent to the user. We'll begin with LANs.

LANS

Geographically, local area networks are the smallest of
the topologies. LANs usually cover an area of less than
one to two miles and operate at speeds of up to 100
Mbps, although today four, 10, and 16 Mbps are most
widely used. LAN technology was first developed in
response to the growing distribution of computing
power in the seventies and eighties. Today, the dramatic
increase in the use of personal computers has created
an unprecedented demand for local communications,
what we referred to in Chapter 9 as "connectivity."

But local connectivity has its barriers. PCs were
designed to be computers, not communication devices;
products from different vendors are not compatible;
and old technologies have created inefficiencies in
existing systems. With previously installed systems,
network response time is often slow, expansion is difficult, adding and moving terminals is a complicated procedure, and network managers end up with a wiring
nightmare resembling the Amazon jungle on a bad day.
LANs solve these problems with the flexibility to connect a variety of equipment to share resources such as
storage devices and printers, share information, and
communicate via electronic mail. The ability to simply
transfer files without having to "sneakernet" floppy
disks around has enamored many a user.

We've described topology as the "design" for
connecting network **nodes** or destinations. In LAN
technology, nodes can be connected physically or logi-
cally. Logical connections are facilitated through rout-

ing, where nodes not physically connected point-to-point can communicate through intermediary devices or nodes. The three major LAN topologies are, in historical order, star, bus and ring.

Star is just what it sounds like. It's a LAN topology in which terminals are connected by lines branching from a central node (figure 10-1). What's obvious is that the central node constitutes a single point of failure, making maintenance either a dream or a nightmare. Expansion is nondisruptive since all the nodes are connected point-to-point, but as you add nodes you embark on a one way trip back into the Amazon, trying to find ways to hide the ever increasing mileage of new cable. In star networks, communication works best between central and outlying nodes rather than among outlying nodes because of the delay incurred passing through the hub.

> In a star topology, terminals are connected by lines branching from a central node.

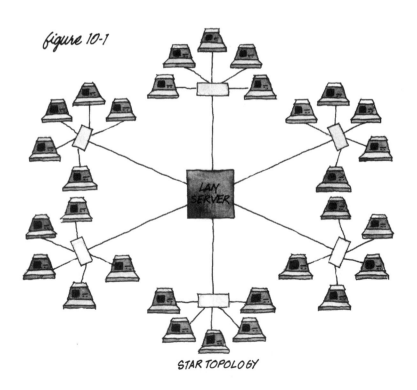

figure 10-1

STAR TOPOLOGY

Bus is also what it sounds like, unless you're expecting something large and yellow with tires. Bus *route* would be more accurate (figure 10-2). In this LAN topology, nodes attach to a physical channel by taps or connectors. **Ethernet,** a common LAN standard, is a good example. Nodes are required to know their own addresses but don't act as repeaters, so they don't add delay. Expansion requires no rewiring, and no single node can bring down the network.

Ring is a LAN topology in which nodes are connected point-to-point forming a circle (figure 10-3). **Token Ring,** an IBM contribution, is one common standard, and is currently challenging the older and more prevalent Ethernet as LANs continue to expand. In a ring topology, the nodes act as repeaters to retransmit messages to other nodes along the ring. Control is distributed, but now, with several points of failure, any one node may bring down the whole network. Expansion also interrupts communications since the ring must be temporarily broken to accommodate the installation of new nodes.

Bus topologies feature LANs attached to a physical channel by taps or connectors.

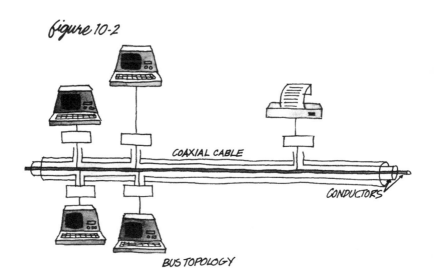

figure 10-2

COAXIAL CABLE

CONDUCTORS

BUS TOPOLOGY

116

The three most common methods of a node trying to get its two cents in (a technical term for the less glamorous "passing data") are polling, token passing, and contention.

In **polling**, the central node, as in a star network, governs communications by offering each node equal access to the network, one at a time. Though it occurs in split seconds, by data communications standards polling is slow. In **token passing**, an access token (bit stream) passes through the LAN. If a node wants to transmit, it inserts a message in front of the bit stream, then reinserts the token back on the network. Because it's speedier and more manageable than its two counterparts, token passing is the fastest growing method of passing data. **Contention** is simply first come, first served and is most often used in bus technologies. (Imagine several people from a major East Coast city all trying to get on a bus at the same time.) An optional feature like *collision detection* introduces a certain politeness into bus loading and ensures that all transmissions eventually get through. Contention has been around longer and therefore is the method used by many large installed bases.

In a ring topology, nodes are connected point-to-point forming a circle.

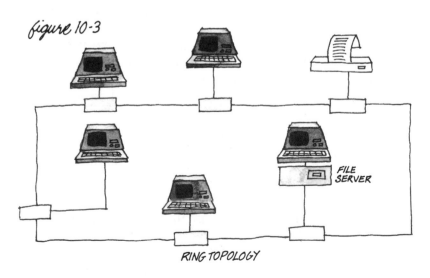

figure 10-3

FILE SERVER

RING TOPOLOGY

Does it seem like things in this chapter keep occurring in threes? Twisted pair wiring, coaxial cable, and fiber optic cable are the four most common LAN media (no, you're right, it's three). Which one gets used depends on several factors, including cost, ease of installation, and whether your connection is to the desktop or to the backbone.

Twisted pair wiring comes in two varieties, shielded and unshielded. **Unshielded twisted pair** telephone wiring (two insulated copper wires wrapped around each other) is already installed in most buildings and is therefore the de facto standard for desktop LAN connections. Unshielded twisted pair wiring is abundant, the least expensive of the three media, and susceptible to electromagnetic waves (remember those flickering fluorescent lights?) and radio interference. **Shielded twisted pair** wiring (which is like unshielded but with an extra layer of insulation) is more expensive but is less susceptible to electromagnetic interference.

Coaxial cable, the medium of cable television, is costlier and more difficult to install than twisted pair wiring. It's also as thick as a fat thumb and not very flexible. However, it's great for data. It offers large bandwidth for volume and speed, high immunity to electrical interference, and low error rate. Coaxial can be used for both baseband and broadband signaling. **Baseband** transmits only data and uses the entire bandwidth for a single digital signal while **broadband** can accommodate data, video and voice using many channels for multiple analog signals. As you may have guessed, broadband is more expensive and complicated to install than baseband.

Fiber optic cabling, sometimes referred to as "glass", is just that. Fine glass filaments conduct light pulses converted from electrical signals. It offers even higher bandwidth, higher immunity from electrical interference, greater security, and a higher price tag (that is already falling fast). Installing fiber, formerly one of its biggest drawbacks, is quickly becoming easier, too, although delicate handling and special connectors are required. All of which makes it ideal for backbone LAN connections. During the next decade, fiber may well challenge unshielded twisted pair wiring as the medium of choice for desktop connections as well.

Now you may have been wondering just how all those nodes and cables get connected. Well, **NICs** and **MAUs** (of course! you say) are the answer. A NIC (Network Interface Card) is a card that goes in the PC/workstation to connect it. MAUs (Media Access Units) let cables connect to other cables (such as backbones) without the need for tools simply by using modular jacks (like that little plug on the end of your phone cord).

And what are these "servers" everyone is talking about? Surely you've heard about "client server architecture"? (And no, it's not marketing hype for a new type of English butler.) The **client** is the PC or workstation on the LAN that accesses the **server**, which is another PC or workstation on the LAN containing a database or applications software shared by many people using the LAN.

LAN INTERCONNECTION DEVICES
You might have guessed it. All these independent LANs one day decide that now they want to talk to each other (LANs have needs too!). This growing need for greater connectivity has fueled the development of LAN interconnection devices. These devices can link local area networks, whether in the same building or different states, allowing users to share resources and information. LAN interconnection needs vary from linking LANs in local environments to linking LANs from different geographical locations using WAN facilities such as DDS, T1, or X.25. *Three* (wouldn't you know it) popular interconnection devices are bridges, routers and gateways.

Bridges connect multiple similar LANS to form a single virtual LAN (figure 10-4). A unique characteristic of bridges is that they're protocol independent. Data can be in any protocol format, such as TCP/IP or DECnet and the bridge "won't care." Bridges don't look at the data or change it in any way, so processing time is reduced, making bridges the fastest of the LAN interconnection methods. They're also often the cheapest to operate, since less horse power is needed.

Remote LAN bridges are used to connect similar LANs in widely scattered locations. Some remote bridges use multiple 56 Kbps DDS links. More efficient ones use Fractional T1 services—that is, increments of 64 Kbps lines, which allows you to connect more logical LANs over a single physical channel. In effect, the bridge "multiplexes" the separate LAN connections, reducing both line costs and port charges (figure 10-5).

A bridge connects multiple LANs of a similar type, while gateways connect dissimilar LANs.

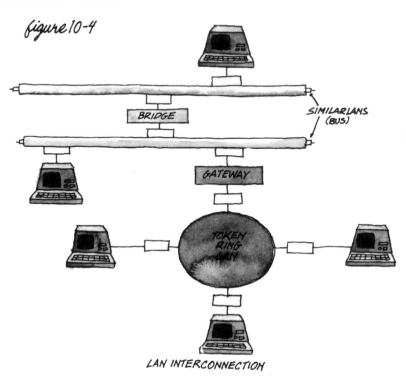

figure 10-4

SIMILAR LANS (BUS)

BRIDGE

GATEWAY

TOKEN RING LAN

LAN INTERCONNECTION

Routers offer more sophisticated features than bridges and can facilitate communication between dissimilar LANs (i.e., Ethernet and token ring) using a common protocol. These devices are protocol sensitive. Routers have added intelligence to choose the transmission route based on the least cost, shortest path, or other programmable factors. In addition, routers offer traffic congestion and flow control. The extra intelligence required, however, impacts router performance and cost as compared with bridges. But because of reduced overhead, routers may offer better efficiency in large complex networks.

A remote LAN bridge with multiplexing capabilities can use Fractional T1 services to connect more logical LANs over a single physical channel.

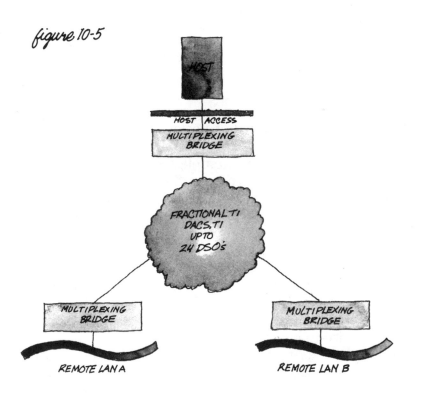

figure 10-5

121

Gateways connect networks running different protocols through protocol conversion—especially LAN-to-WAN or LAN-to-host connections (figure 10-4). This means users of different network architectures such as SNA, DECnet, TCP/IP and X.25 can finally talk to one another because the gateway acts as translator. In contrast, routers look at data and only route the data to a network using the same protocol. Gateway performance can be explained in relation to the OSI Reference Model (figure 9-3). While bridges operate at Layer 2 and routers operate at Layer 3, gateways use all seven layers of the model to make even the most seemingly impossible connections possible. Users on OSI-based networks need not be isolated from users on proprietary architecture-based networks. But because of the increased processing overhead involved in operations like "language translation", gateways tend to be even slower than routers.

We probably don't need to point out (but we can't resist the temptation) that in determining which LAN interconnection device is most appropriate for your needs, price/performance is probably the key factor. The basic information provided above should help you ask some of the right questions.

Because a major goal of a LAN is to connect varied systems together, standards are continually being developed to specify rules of communications. We've discussed the efforts of the ISO briefly in Chapter 1. Vendors have also attempted to develop networking standards through product offerings. We've already met two of these standards. One is Ethernet (known to close friends as **IEEE 802.3**), which specifies a particular LAN topology, medium and data rate. The other is Token Ring, which also goes by the standard name of **IEEE 802.5**.

The growing appeal of fiber is also reflected in a new standard called **FDDI** (Fiber Distributed Data Interface). FDDI is a high-speed fiber optic networking standard that conforms to the ISO's OSI model. Defined by the American National Standards Institute (ANSI), the U.S. representative to the ISO, FDDI spe-

122

cifies a 100 Mbps network using fiber optic cabling. FDDI provides more LAN bandwidth for increasingly image-based applications. It allows users to connect LANs over large areas. Its dual ring topology makes it capable of operating around a cable break or node failure. And its support by all leading networking companies make it likely to become the dominant LAN networking standard of the 1990s.

MANS

Think of MANs (metropolitan area networks) as city-wide LANs, making large scale LAN resource sharing possible. In fact, MAN technology originally evolved from LAN designs. It uses digital backbones, specifically fiber optics, to carry traffic, link WANs and support applications such as high-speed file transfer, video conferencing, and integrated data, voice, and text. Where LANs are best at short distance resource sharing and broadcast access, and WANS in general provide distance but limited speed and efficiency when dealing with bursty communications, MANs function as a performance and feature bridge between the two, as well as a data communications bridge.

There are six very definite points to be made about metropolitan area networks: They're public, not private networks. They're switched, offering packet and virtual-circuit switching. They're tied together by fiber optic cable. The bandwidth starts at 45 Mbps. They must be integrated, with a single-switch matrix for different speeds and services. And they don't exist. We're not kidding. But don't worry, the reports of their non-existence are greatly exaggerated. MANs are sure to be introduced over the next few years and are already being trial-tested by several Bell Operating Companies. Let us explain.

The demand for high speed connectivity is driving all kinds of new technologies. The explosion of LANs and WANs is an excellent illustration and that, incidentally, is where the growth has been in data communications. LANs and WANs are usually private networks. The development of MAN technology is being driven by local public telephone companies to meet the demand for local and metropolitan connectivity.

Historically, the local telephone companies have been weak in providing the "cutting edge" features to attract large users. In an effort to participate in the LAN-to-LAN and LAN-to-WAN connection, render services, and secure a niche as the "middlemen" of connectivity, local phone companies are introducing MANs. As a public networking solution, MANs are expected to be an easy way of connecting LANs, plus they'll offer a cost savings when compared to setting up private networks.

What is a MAN? (You're expecting a joke, aren't you?) A MAN consists of dedicated high-speed packet switches. A MAN is also not a great conversationalist. Though many out there would agree, this is actually in the specifications. MAN traffic initially will not carry voice but will share the communication paths in a local exchange carrier's **SONET** (Synchronous Optical Network)-based fiber optic transport plan. SONET is a standard interface designed to bring increased uniformity and new capabilities to fiber optic transmission. Based on light wave technology, speeds range from 50 Mbps to nearly 2,500 Mbps. The benefits include faster access to new services, extra network capacity on demand, and instant recovery from network failures.

Initial MAN interfaces will be DS3 and DS1. Higher and lower speed interfaces will come later to support a wider range of applications. MANs will initially connect to users via T1 links and bridging technology, later over standard interfaces which connect similar LANs, and still later over connections with protocol conversion for dissimilar LANs. When MANs are fully implemented, they'll offer WAN connectivity through links to the long distance carriers.

Now for the big words. **Switched Multimegabit Data Service (SMDS)** is the Bell companies' commercial adoption of the **IEEE 802.6** MAN standard which was pioneered by QPSX (Queued Packet Synchronous Exchange). QPSX is both an architecture and a company—probably confusing for employees. QPSX, the company, designed the architecture behind the MAN standard and licenses the design to other organizations. (To make things even more confusing, the architecture QPSX is now called **DQDB—Distributed Queued Dual Bus**—by the IEEE 802.6 group.) SMDS's potential as a LAN interconnect service is already recognized by the telephone companies, and internetworking equipment manufacturers are coordinating their efforts for equipment compatibility to the SMDS service. In time, higher bandwidth services including broadband ISDN will be available as the local phone companies install more fiber and sophisticated switching equipment.

WANS

You may be thinking, "Tell me something I don't already know." We can't. Since Chapters 1 through 9 have been devoted to WAN technology, there's really nothing more to say here. You already know it all. School's out. Well, just about.

If you've been applying some of the technologies we've been discussing in the last few chapters, your network has evolved into quite a complex, invaluable corporate asset. In the introduction, we said that even the best networks go down. Your equipment may not even be responsible—it could be a tornado in Toledo tore up your leased lines. Tornado or not, when your network is down, so is your business.

Have you ever thought about what you'll say if your terminal user comes running in like the lookout on the Titanic to tell you his screen just went blank and he can't transmit or receive data? Well think about it, because it could very well happen. And however long it takes you to get your system up and running again is measured not only in time but in money as well. Hint: As of this writing, major airlines lose $20,000 a minute when they experience a major network outage. Ouch.

11

NETWORK MANAGEMENT OR

when the chips are down

In the old days. . . Twenty years ago, when you thought computers, you thought IBM. When you wanted telephone equipment, you called AT&T. And when you put together a network, all you needed was a set of modems.

We don't mean to make it sound as simple as playing telephone with two wax cups and a string, but there wasn't the range of equipment, varied applications and choice of vendors available today.

Networks expanded and modems began evolving into "smarter," more advanced devices capable of performing some basic diagnostic tests. These tests were especially useful during times of network difficulty. The data communications manager would attempt to determine a network problem from studying the modems' indicator lights. Otherwise, highly trained technicians carting cumbersome test equipment were sent to remote locations to try to isolate and remedy the situation.

As networks started evolving into more complex systems, the data communications manager was beginning to experience some network difficulty of his own. It was fast becoming impossible to keep track of all the flashing lights and the status of the line conditions while all the time manually logging observations in a notebook that represented the "database" of network performance. Under these conditions, the data communications manager's view of the network was, at best, piecemeal and fragmented.

What was the procedure for dealing with the inevitable network failures? Let's say you were the person in charge of the network. Usually you were first alerted to a network problem by a user unable to access the host from his terminal. Since downtime means lost business and lost money, communications had to be restored as soon as possible. But was the failure in the phone line or in the equipment? And if it was the equipment, which vendor's equipment?

Running to your Rolodex,™ you started making phone calls to the phone company and various vendors. Of course, service technicians weren't always available so it might have been several hours before testing to isolate the failure began.

"Finger-pointing" between the carrier and vendors and even among vendors was standard procedure. After the most extensive testing, the problem always seemed to be in the other guy's equipment.

Several hours later, you were no closer to resolving the network problem, the only thing that was flowing out of your business was money, and you wished you'd taken that night course in riot control because your employees were beginning to panic.

At that point, you might have had a wild fantasy of decreasing your dependence on the carrier and independent vendors for diagnosing your communications problems, and taking control of your own network.

If this scenario hasn't convinced you of the need for centralized, automated network control, there's more.

Today the network has become a strategic corporate asset. Users are demanding greater throughput and response time which, of course, means increased network availability. Downtime is becoming less and less affordable. The faster a downed network can be brought back up, the more money is saved.

All of which brings us to the need for centralized network management. But first, a bit of background.

A FIRST STEP: NETWORK CONTROL

In the mid-1970s, leading modem vendors (including, of course, Codex) began offering tools for testing network functions and diagnosing problems. Building on the capabilities of those "smart" modems that the datacomm manager had come to treasure, these tools consisted of a central device that communicated with all of the compatible modems in the network. This "shadow network" sent and received its signals over the same phone lines that were used for transmitting "real" data. How? By means of time division multiplexing, which, as we've seen, creates a second, low-speed data channel alongside the main data channel.

This was a big step forward. These new tools—generally known as **network control systems** or **NCS**—gave datacomm managers their first comprehensive look at their networks. And because these new-found diagnostic capabilities tended to produce pretty clear indications of where a problem lay, fingerpointing among vendors was greatly reduced.

Diagnosis, then, was a key function of the NCS. But what about "control"? In fact, a subset of these network control systems delivered what they promised: the ability to "control" the network by solving problems from the central location. Sometimes this involved a simple intervention, such as changing from one piece of equipment to a backup device. At other times, it involved a long-distance "reconfiguration," or reprogramming, of a troublesome component in the network.

Again, this is good stuff, and network users liked it. To no one's surprise, the giant mainframe manufacturers took steps to avoid getting left behind. (IBM, for one, followed a slightly different route from the modem manufacturers. Big Blue already had a major investment in diagnostics for its central computers, and these diagnostics were based on a scheme whereby control signals were "tucked into" the main data channel, along with the user's data stream. So when IBM extended its network control capabilities outward from its mainframe and front-end processors, it retained this original design, rather than going the multiplexing route.)

Truth be told, though, none of these NCS schemes were perfect. For one thing, although they handled modems more or less adequately, they didn't necessarily deal with other network components: multiplexers, switches, and so on. Furthermore, their user interfaces tended to be clunky and unfriendly. On a bad day, you might still hear that mournful cry echoing down the halls: "What's going *on* out there?" And because the systems were awkward to use, they tended not to get used enough. For example: if adding new network devices to the control system's "registry" of hardware was cumbersome, well, maybe it just didn't get done.

Just as troubling was the fact that these network control systems were mainly designed to help users react to problems. They weren't very good at analyzing how whatever had just happened fit into any larger picture. They were of very little use in spotting a minor problem, such as a slowly degrading phone line, before it turned into a major problem. They couldn't spot and flag the subtle, submerged operational trends that sometimes turn out to be Problems-in-the-Making.

Clearly, a new and more sophisticated generation of network control devices was needed. In the early to mid-1980s, this new generation began to emerge, with a new name: **network management systems** or **NMS**.

NETWORK MANAGEMENT SYSTEMS

The trend of top management to look at the communications network as a corporate asset fueled the expansion of the NCS into the NMS. What exactly does the ideal network management system do? Let's see.

The recognition that the network is a strategic corporate asset fueled the expansion of the network control system into the network management system.

Traditionally, the NMS incorporated all the features of an NCS but added a management database element to organize, analyze and predict network faults and trends. In this way, management is provided with regular statistical reports and detailed summaries from collected diagnostics to aid in evaluating network performance and future planning.

Today, for fairly straightforward modem or modem/multiplexer networks, basic NMSs still provide a cost-effective network management solution. However, when you attempt to integrate all the technologies and products we've been discussing since Chapter 4— in other words, your entire wide area network—the job quickly becomes unmanageable with conventional systems. To administer complex hybrid networks, basic control and diagnostics are simply no longer enough.

That's because ideally you want to be able to manage *all* your wide area network devices, including modems, DSU/CSUs, T1/E1 muxes, and X.25 concentrators and switches, and LAN interconnection devices from a central location. You want the flexibility to accommodate new technologies that are sure to come along in the future. And although we'd like to think you'd choose one vendor for your full range of products (guess which!), we realize you probably use a mix of vendor products to acquire the technologies that best suit your applications.

To state the challenge another way, the ideal network management system should provide you with a common user interface, database, inventory mechanism, and alarm reporting and control scheme for different classes of devices as well as interfaces to systems which do what it doesn't.

Well, vendors *have* developed techniques for **integrating** *most* of your network elements under *one* management system. The key is advanced **software architecture**. (Yes, that word "advanced" does get thrown around a lot, doesn't it, but in this software-driven age, advances are made so rapidly that we decided it best to play it safe and go with a vague word that connotes a sound general idea rather than a specific word that might become dated the day after tomorrow.)

Today's software architecture allows network management systems to provide more information, faster and more accessibly than ever before.

So. . . applying this advanced architecture to management system design results in more information being provided—faster and more accessibly than ever before. Color graphics, maps, menus, and windowing make these systems easy to use, and the ability of the same user interface to manage all network components increases productivity and greatly reduces training time. These systems present a flexible, topological view that allows you to monitor the entire network or **view** (subset) of the network by geographic location, device type, network application, or other criteria.

What kinds of applications does such a system perform? These fall into two categories: operational and administrative.

Fault management is one of the chief applications in the operational group. That's the effort to identify and diagnose network problems quickly and efficiently—so that they can be promptly resolved. It usually involves a series of tests, designed to give an ever more precise picture of what's going on in the network and thereby to isolate the problem. If your system provides **time-based testing,** tests can even be scheduled to run automatically while you attend to other tasks. This entire scenario presupposes some **thresholds**, which you yourself set in order to define "trouble" any way you need to. An added benefit in most NMSs is **trouble ticketing**—the creation of a database library of problems and their resolutions.

Configuration management, another operational application, comprises two major activities: inventory management, which profiles all the objects in the network, and topology management, which shows you how those objects are connected and allows you to reconnect them in new ways. The most helpful systems allow you to manipulate the device parameter settings and change the operational characteristics of the network right from your NMS screen. Configuration management also includes system implementation planning tools, allowing you to enter topology and inventory information for devices not yet installed—in other words, to pre-configure before a device really exists!

Performance measurement straddles the line between operational and administrative functions. For example, some systems monitor the key analog line parameters that affect data transmission so that you can track line performance and notify your telco of any ongoing problems. Collecting this information over time facilitates various administrative and planning activities.

Other applications representing the administrative functions of an effective NMS include **accounting management** and the various levels of **security** guarding access to both the NMS itself and the devices in the network.

Such a system obviously serves as a key strategic **planning** tool as well. Information collected about the network can be made available for performance and trend analysis, to help you realize the maximum return on your network investment. For instance, a node assumed to be carrying the heaviest traffic may turn out to be the lightest. Network resources can then be redeployed to add extra bandwidth without increasing costs. So you can see how an integrated network management system pays for itself.

We've chosen to focus here on wide area network management, because WANs are the primary focus of this book. But what about **LAN managers?** And those so-called **SuperManagers** designed by the big computer companies and carriers? Briefly, LAN managers perform the network management function for the local area network. But few are the companies with just one LAN. As we saw in the last chapter, more and more LANs are communicating across the wide area network. So effective WAN management—including management of LAN interconnection devices—becomes increasingly critical to the smooth integration and operation of these disparate LANs.

Effective wide area network (WAN) management—including management of LAN interconnection devices—is critical to the smooth operation of disparate LANs.

And what about SuperManagers? Well, they *are* impressive, combining as they do management data from multiple vendors' equipment into a common database. The trade-off is that they support the least common denominator among all those vendors' products. OK, admittedly that's a little vague. Think of it this way: if a SuperManager can integrate the same 20% of every vendor's system, then that's providing a very valuable function. However, what do you use for the other 80%?

The truth is that no single network management system out there today can do it all. Which brings us back to the subject of standards—a running theme of this book since Chapter 1. As you'll remember, standards are critical because they facilitate integration, flexibility, and choice.

Vendors using OSI standards, for example,will be able to ensure interoperability between open systems and network management products. (Consider dipping back into Chapter 9 if you need an OSI refresher.) The only alternative is strategic partnering and joint development among vendors and even competitors.

Many OSI management recommendations have already reached standards status. A number of others are nearing completion. The first to pass were Common Management Information Protocol/Common Management Information Services (**CMIP/CMIS**). These ensure that OSI management systems will recognize one another's commands because protocols and services will be the same.

While all the relevant pieces of OSI are being put in place, a number of other nonproprietary standards have emerged on the scene. The most important of these is the **Simple Network Management Protocol (SNMP),** which has become the de facto standard until OSI is ready for full implementation. SNMP permits some degree of interoperability, particularly on the LAN-management level. A number of vendors have incorporated SNMP in their products in the belief that SNMP will be easily convertible to CMIP when the time comes.

With much of the work already accomplished, the prospect for network management and software that will link different vendors and their products is looking better every day. For more details—a lot more details—on network management, check out our *Basics Book of Network Management.*

IS YOUR NETWORK UNDERINSURED?

The treatment of network problems has come a long way, from hauling test equipment to remote sites, to sitting at a console reading a report on current network trends.

Perhaps you feel your network application isn't critical enough to justify the cost of a network management system. The bottom line is, how much money will you lose if your network goes down? And how long can you afford to have it down? Trying to figure out the probabilities of such a failure is unimportant if you can't afford the downtime to begin with.

Now the good news. You've just finished eleven chapters of this book and you understand enough about information networking not only to talk confidently about the subject, but also to get your own network up and running!

INFORMATION NETWORKING APPLICATIONS

OR

configuring things out

Now's the time to really sit back, put your feet up and enjoy this book, because Chapter 12 is going to tie together everything you've learned since page one. Consider it an open book test with the answers included.

Using an automotive analogy (for the last time)—it's as if we've been pointing out individual engine parts while building a motor. Now you're about to see what happens when we turn the key.

Using network diagrams and captions, the following pages illustrate many of the concepts we've been discussing. The more complex diagrams are nothing more than a combination of a few simple networking ideas and are easy to "sound out."

1. Short-haul application.

The long-haul network of a financial services company spans from San Francisco to New York, where it terminates at a multiplexer in corporate headquarters. From there, limited distance modems deliver a range of different, cost-effective solutions to meet specific short-haul needs.

Some LDMs, running on company-installed twisted-pair wiring, transmit both sync and async data to terminals and workstations on various floors. Other LDMs transmit data at 19.2 Kbps full-duplex to the company's nearby product operations division.

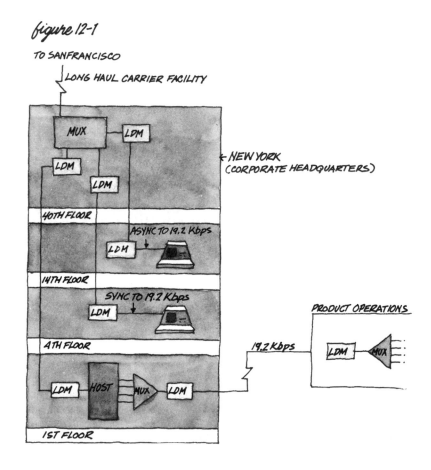

figure 12-1

2. Long distance dial network.

A regional sales director in Dallas must send forecasting figures to the vice president of sales based at company headquarters in Hartford. Since the required connect time is never more than five hours a week, the most cost-effective solution is to use two personal computers (asynchronous terminals) with standard communications software packages, and two 2400 bps dial modems, connected via the dial network.

The salesman in Dallas occasionally needs to access the Compuserve and Dow Jones databases. From his PC, the salesman can use his same 2400 bps dial modem to call into the databases over the dial network. Since users dialing into the databases use modems of different speeds, both databases use V.22 bis modems. V.22 bis has the flexibility to adjust to caller inbound rates of 300, 1200 and 2400 bps.

The host computer in Hartford down-line loads information to Point Of Sale (POS) terminals in each of the twenty-five branch stores. Since this requires limited connect time, information is transmitted during the evening over the dial network when tariff rates are reduced. The host sends information synchronously using its 2400 bps dial modem to the POS terminals via their 2400 bps modems.

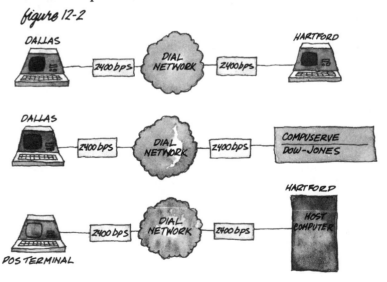

figure 12-2

3. How point-to-point networks become . . .

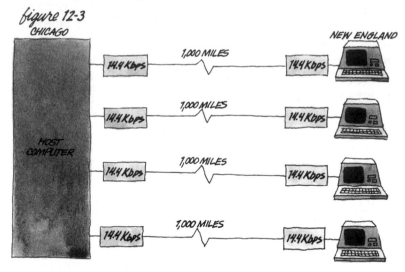

figure 12-3

. . . a single multipoint network.

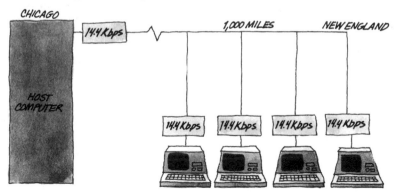

All four New England branch offices of a large company frequently need to access their host computer in Chicago. The frequent transmissions required between New England and Chicago make dial lines uneconomical. But a series of leased point-to-point connections from Chicago to New England would total 4,000 miles of leased lines and require four computer ports at the central facility.

Since the data communications needs of all four branches are so similar, they're able to share a single computer port. This is accomplished by reducing the network to a single leased line and using multipoint modems. This eliminates the 3,000 miles of communication lines required in the point-to-point scenario. Addressable terminals and high-speed synchronous, multipoint modems meet the requirements of this configuration. The multipoint modems operate at an outbound rate of 14.4 Kbps and an inbound rate of 9600 bps.

4. Multipoint, multiprotocol network.

X.25 packet switching products save money by reducing the resources needed to handle diverse applications. For example, in this banking situation, three applications—teller terminal, ATM, and security, each using a different protocol—were being run over three separate lines. By turning to a multipoint, multiprotocol packet solution, they were able to consolidate these applications over one line, reducing line costs. Today some branches are replacing their teller terminals with LANs, which are also readily accommodated by the new network.

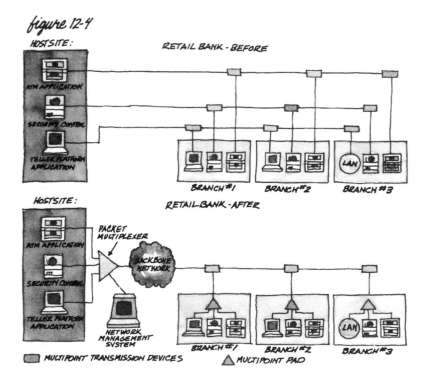

figure 12-4

HOST SITE: RETAIL BANK - BEFORE

ATM APPLICATION
SECURITY CONTROL
TELLER PLATFORM APPLICATION

BRANCH #1   BRANCH #2   BRANCH #3

HOST SITE: RETAIL BANK - AFTER

ATM APPLICATION
SECURITY CONTROL
TELLER PLATFORM APPLICATION

PACKET MULTIPLEXER
BACKBONE NETWORK
NETWORK MANAGEMENT SYSTEM

BRANCH #1   BRANCH #2   BRANCH #3

▭ MULTIPOINT TRANSMISSION DEVICES   △ MULTIPOINT PAD

5. Digital bridge operating as a modem sharing unit.

The Philadelphia headquarters of a company is connected to a synchronous terminal in the Pittsburgh sales office via a leased line and two 2400 bps modems. Now, two more synchronous terminals need to be added to the Pittsburgh office.

One solution would be to configure a polled multipoint network. This is fine, but costs can be reduced even further in this case. Because all three terminals are located in the same office, they can share the line using a digital bridge. This eliminates two 2400 bps modems. The company still has a cost-effective multipoint network, and the host operates through the digital bridge to poll the three terminals individually.

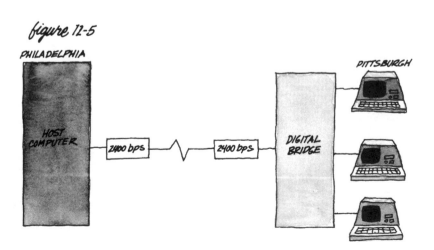

figure 12-5

PHILADELPHIA

PITTSBURGH

HOST COMPUTER · 2400 bps — 2400 bps · DIGITAL BRIDGE

6. Digital bridge facilitating digital network backup.

Let's say you're running a digital network. What happens when the digital lines go down? Assuming that the backup required averages less than three hours a day, you could use an analog dial backup system via digital bridges that's able to handle high speeds like 9600 bps. These high-speed dial modems (which conform to the CCITT's V.32 recommendation) will back up only the line that has gone down—eliminating the need for a mirror image leased line analog system. And best of all, dial lets you route around a site that is off-line without interruption to your network.

figure 12-6

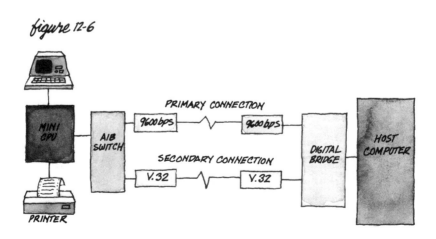

7. 19.2 Kbps multiplexed modems.

A company based in Boston has sales offices in London, Amsterdam, Paris, and Tokyo. To connect each of the sales offices individually with the Atlanta host would require eight modems, creating four point-to-point lines adding up to approximately 16,900 miles of phone line.

Using multiplexers would be one solution. But since all four terminals are synchronous, there's a less expensive way— a pair of 19.2 Kbps modems. These six-channel, buffered multiplexed modems reduce the leased line requirements by 7,250 miles.

The built-in buffered mux allows the modems to handle a mix of synchronous transmissions operating at different speeds. The only constraint is that the sum of all speeds must be equal to or less than 19.2 Kbps. So Tokyo can transmit at 9600 bps, and Amsterdam at 2400 bps, while Paris transmits at 4800 bps.

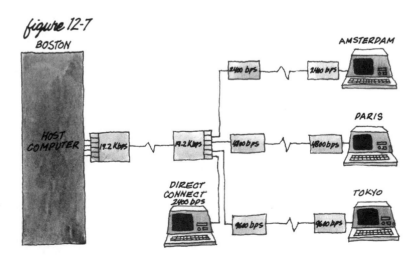

figure 12-7

BOSTON

AMSTERDAM

PARIS

TOKYO

HOST COMPUTER

DIRECT CONNECT 2400 bps

8. Before multiplexing a network . . .

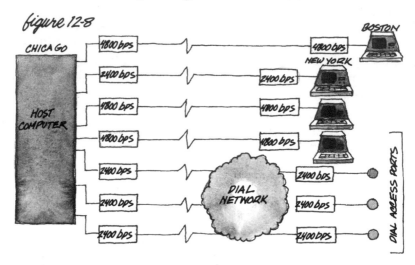

figure 12-8

. . . and after multiplexing.

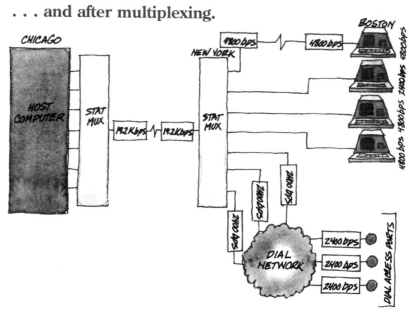

There are three terminals in New York City and one in Boston, with each one linked point-to-point to the host computer in Chicago. The addition of two statistical multiplexers, however, eliminates nearly three quarters of the point-to-point leased lines, increases network flexibility and boosts data throughput.

The Boston terminal connects to the stat muxes by a 4800 bps tail circuit. Other terminals in New York are linked to the host via dial access ports, reducing long distance dial call charges to local call charges.

The stat muxes can also handle a variety of terminal speeds as well as a mix of synchronous and asynchronous data. And because the stat muxes dynamically allocate bandwidth on a demand basis, the sum of the terminals' transmission speeds can exceed the transmission rate of the high-speed link.

9. Frame relay network.

Engineering design groups, one in Detroit and one in Lansing, Michigan, are working together on a project, using CAD/CAM to develop an engine. Engineers in the groups communicate several times a day with each other over the network backbone. They frequently share information regarding the product's specifications and design with two manufacturing groups, one in a Detroit suburb and one in Munich, Germany. In addition, all the groups send weekly updates about the project's progress to headquarters in downtown Chicago.

In the past, multiple lines had to be deployed from the X.25 packet switches and the LAN routers to the fast packet nodes to achieve end-to-end connectivity between all the end points and allow each location to communicate with all the others. This resulted in a bottleneck when engineers and managers on LANs tried to move data onto the backbone at the same time. Transmission delay was long, because there was no network access protocol capable of effectively handling the bursty, unpredictable data traffic generated from the LANs. Development slowed and employees became frustrated.

When frame relay was combined with fast packet on the network, the network could handle the bursty, unpredictable traffic from the LANs. Productivity between the work groups jumped as response time on the network dropped substantially. By providing a single-line interface between end points and relying on end-user devices to handle most of the error processing, frame relay eliminated many lines, dramatically reduced hardware costs, simplified network design, and maximized bandwidth availability. The bottom line: it saved money.

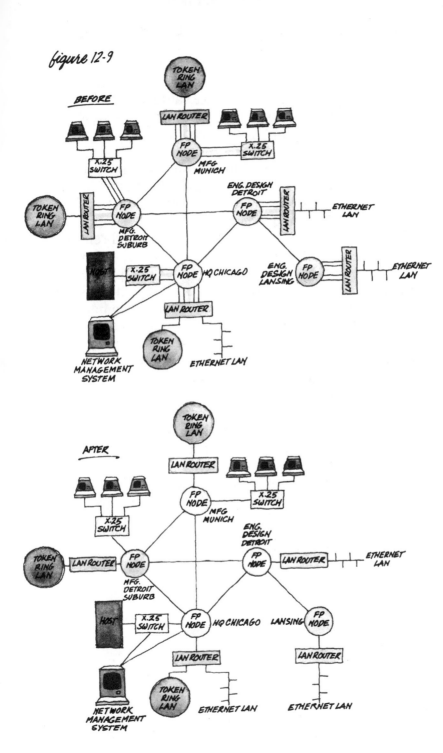

figure 12-9

BEFORE

TOKEN RING LAN

LAN ROUTER

FP NODE

MFG. MUNICH

X.25 SWITCH

TOKEN RING LAN

LAN ROUTER

FP NODE

MFG. DETROIT SUBURB

X.25 SWITCH

ENG. DESIGN DETROIT

FP NODE

LAN ROUTER

ETHERNET LAN

HOST

X.25 SWITCH

FP NODE   HQ CHICAGO

ENG. DESIGN LANSING

FP NODE

LAN ROUTER

ETHERNET LAN

LAN ROUTER

TOKEN RING LAN

ETHERNET LAN

NETWORK MANAGEMENT SYSTEM

AFTER

TOKEN RING LAN

LAN ROUTER

FP NODE

MFG. MUNICH

X.25 SWITCH

TOKEN RING LAN

LAN ROUTER

FP NODE

MFG. DETROIT SUBURB

ENG. DESIGN DETROIT

FP NODE

LAN ROUTER

ETHERNET LAN

HOST

X.25 SWITCH

FP NODE   HQ CHICAGO

LANSING

FP NODE

LAN ROUTER

NETWORK MANAGEMENT SYSTEM

TOKEN RING LAN

ETHERNET LAN

LAN ROUTER

ETHERNET LAN

10. Network management for typically complex networks.

The previous applications are fairly simple and quite often are actually part of much larger networks. In Chapter 11, we talked about the value of network management and the importance of standards so that one network management system can operate with a range of products.

In this case, we're looking at a private voice and data network. This could be a typical manufacturing application. It's basically an X.25 network with a T1 backbone, all managed from the Chicago central site. The data carried between headquarters and remote offices includes inventory, shipping, sales, and pricing information. The Atlanta site is where the product is warehoused. The bandwidth afforded by the T1s will support voice as well as data. The PADs can handle SDLC and X.25 protocols. The X.25 Packet Switched Data Network (PSDN) provides international communications with European distributors.

In terms of vendor equipment and diverse technologies, this looks like a three ring circus. Yet the network manager has assembled the best technologies for these particular applications. And from the network management console, our user has end-to-end visibility of the network from the Chicago headquarters to the remote nodes. Any problems can be monitored, diagnosed, and often times remedied without remote on-site intervention. Network availability is maximized, the business enjoys nonstop communications, and this, after all, is what information networking is all about.

figure 12-10

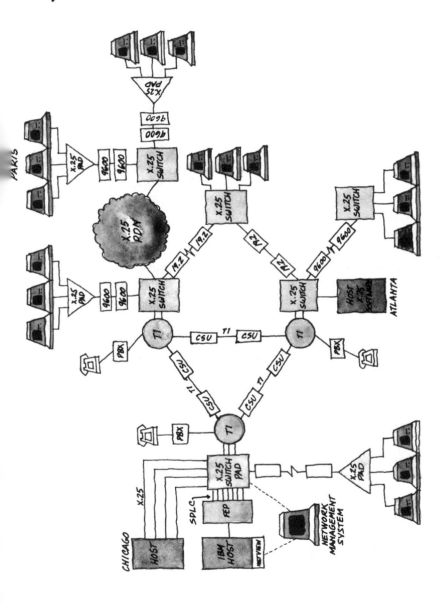

11. Managed high-speed dial network.

In this HMO comprising several thousand doctors, the doctors' offices imprint a subscriber card and transmit to the host for billing purposes. At the host site, a dial modem pool responds to incoming calls. Speed and accuracy are essential.

The pool consists of V.32 bis modems, which can boost speeds to 14.4 Kbps in synchronous applications. In async applications, such as this one, V.32 bis combined with V.42 bis data compression can increase speeds to 38.4 Kbps. In this example, the modems are also backward compatible with the installed base of lower-speed modems in some doctors' offices and with a wide range of error correction schemes.

The dial management system constantly monitors the utilization of the dial pool, identifying bottlenecks and relieving rotary congestion. It eliminates ring-no-answer problems by automatically or manually taking faulty modems out of service. It improves network efficiency by identifying overtime calls. And it provides valuable historical information to help anticipate problems and plan for future expansion.

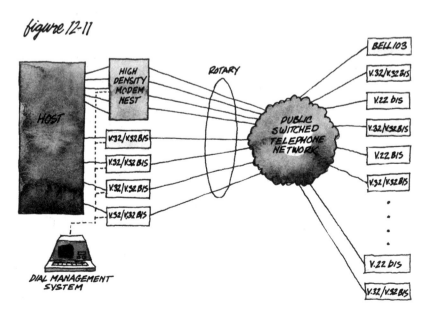

figure 12-11

STANDARDS ORGANIZATIONS

Abbreviation	Name/Location	Standards Discussed In This Book (See index for page references)
ANSI	American National Standards Institute (New York)	FDDI Frame Relay
CCITT	Consultative Committee on International Telephony and Telegraphy (Geneva)	V.22 bis V.24/V.28 V.27 V.29 V.32 V.32 bis V.33 V.35 HDLC ISDN X.21 X.21 bis X.25 Frame Relay
EIA	Electronic Industries Association (Washington, D.C.)	EIA 232-D EIA 530 RS 232-C
IEEE	Institute of Electrical and Electronics Engineers (New York)	IEEE 802.3 IEEE 802.5 IEEE 802.6
ISO	International Organization for Standardization (Geneva)	ASCII OSI Reference Model

ACKNOWLEDGMENT

We'd like to say thank you to all the people who have added their input over the years, helped to work out the bugs, and put the bits and pieces together along the way. But most of all, we'd like to thank the readers, whose great interest has made the book so successful.

CHARTS AND DIAGRAMS

155

INDEX

A
accounting management 133
acoustic couplers 45
adaptive rate system (ARS) 53
amplitude modulation 50
analog bridge 61
ANSI 122
answer modems 46
ASCII 24
asymmetrical multipoint modems 62
asynchronous-to-synchronous
  converter 53
asynchronous transmission 13, 27
auto-answering 52
auto-call 52
automatic adaptive equalizers 52

B
backbone 83
baseband 22, 118
basic rate interface (BRI) 97
baud rate 22
Baudot 23
Bell-compatible modems 46
BISYNC 29
bit 21
bit rate 22
block 22
block check characters 26
bridges 120
broadband 22, 118
buffers 17
bus (LAN topology) 116
byte 22

C
CCITT 41
CCITT-compatible modems 47
character 22
circuit switching 100
CMIP/CMIS 135
coaxial cable 118
computer port 59
conditioning 32
configuration management 133
contention 117
cyclic redundancy check 25

D
D4 frame and format 85
data communications equipment
  (DCE) 2
data compression 73
data service unit/channel service
  unit (DSU/CSU) 79

data terminal equipment (DTE) 2
DDS 80
demodulate 3
dial backup 34, 52
dial line 33
digital bridge 62
distributed queued dual bus
  (DQDB) 125
dropouts 36
DSD (see digital bridge)
dual dial 34
dumb terminals 13

E
E1 82
EBCDIC 23
echo cancellation 53
EIA 40
EIA 232-D 40
EIA 530 41
envelope delay 35
equalizers 51
error-checking 14
Ethernet 116
extended superframe (ESF) 87

F
fast packet technology 89
fault management 133
fiber distributed data interface
  (FDDI) 122
fiber optic cabling 118
fiber optics 78
four-wire 7
fractional T1 87
frame relay 93·
framing 85
frequency division multiplexing
  (FDM) 68
frequency modulation 49
frequency response 35
frequency shift 36
full-duplex 8

G
gain hits 36
gateways 122

H
half-duplex 7
harmonic distortion 36
HDLC 30
horizontal parity 25

I
IEEE 802.3 122
IEEE 802.5 122

156